Why Am I Here?

A Handbook for the Human Experience

Mike Marable

Copyright © 2017 by Mike Marable

All rights reserved. No part of this publication may be reproduced, distributed, or transmitted in any form or by any means, without prior written permission.

Why am I here? A Handbook for the Human Experience /Mike Marable. — 1st ed.

ISBN: 978-1546970590

Library of Congress Control Number: 2017912671

Mike: https://www.mikemarable.com

Email: mike@mikemarable.com

Follow on Twitter: @mikemarablebook

Dedication

This book is dedicated to all the adventurous souls who volunteered to come to our planet at this particular time in history to lend a hand. At times the ride will get bumpy. However, it is those bumps that will also wake us up.

Acknowledgements

This book is a result of thirty years of research. I've had the luxury of having access to information provided by some of the great minds in the fields of psychology, medicine and science. I want to acknowledge these men and women who had the courage to conduct scholarly research into many of the topics discussed in this book which, for many of them, meant having to endure ridicule from their professional peers and, in some cases, it cost them their careers.

Their perseverance and dedication in the pursuit of answers to some of life's most perplexing questions about why we humans are here, our true nature and what happens when we die, is some of the most important research ever conducted, in my opinion. As human beings, we are hardwired to search for the truth about our origins, our purpose and what happens to us when we leave this life. Both religion and science evolved out of the need to satisfy these questions.

The nexus of science and spirituality is a natural communion, since both exist to help explain the biggest mysteries the universe has to offer. Below is a partial list of those who helped me better understand my own experiences. They have dedicated their lives to advancing our understanding of the nature of consciousness and the human experience, to the benefit of all who ask, *"Why am I here?"*

Edgar Mitchell
Wayne Dyer, Ph.D.
Elizabeth Kubler Ross, M.D.
Brian Weiss, M.D.
Jim B. Tucker, M.D.
Ian Stevenson, M.D.
Bruce Greyson, M.D.
Eben Alexander, M.D.
Melvin Morris, M.D.
Gary Zukav
Stuart Hameroff, M.D.
Harold Puthoff, Ph.D.
Raymond Moody, M.D.

Stanislav Grof, Ph.D.
Christina Grof, Ph.D.
Scott Sparrow, Ph.D.
Lee Sannella, M.D.
Anita Moorjani
Stephen LaBerge, M.D.
Robert Monroe
Gary E. Schwartz, Ph.D.
Marianne Williamson
Kenneth Ring, Ph.D.
Jean Houston, Ph.D.
B. J. Miller, M.D.
Atul Gawande, M.D.

A special acknowledgement for Ms. Oprah Winfrey, who has dedicated her career to lending a huge media platform to advance many of the topics presented in this book. Hundreds of millions of people over the years were introduced to some of the most influential people on this list and she helped raise the world's consciousness, as only Oprah can.

An Extraordinary Adventure
Drawing reproduced from The Story of Life by Luigi and Kate Agnelli
www.landk.it

Life is an extraordinary adventure and we are all acrobats and tightrope walkers hanging on to a rope, a dream, an ideal...

We need to be united to be happy, in spite of the bad things in life and the dangers that surround us every day.

Only if we are united can we admire the world, which opens out underneath us in an extraordinary adventure, as in perfect equilibrium we walk towards our dreams and the Neverland!

Signed by two dreamers
Luigi & Kate

Why Am I Here?
A Handbook for the Human Experience

Dedication i
Acknowledgements ii
Introduction vii
We Are All Connected 1
An Awakening Humanity 6
Spooky Science 16
Big Questions 23
Our Search for Answers 26
Where Do I Come From? 30
Rules of the Game 33
Perception, Belief, and Reality 40
The Non-locality of Consciousness 46
You Are Dreaming 52
The Illusion of Time 59
Why am I Here? 63
Writing Our Stories 70
The Mirror of Relationships 75
The End Game 81
Can You Help a Brother (Planet) Out? 89
Epilogue 96
Helpful Terminology 97
Additional Resources 101
ABOUT THE AUTHOR 102

Introduction

*Before enlightenment; chopping wood and carrying water.
After enlightenment; chopping wood and carrying water.*

~ a Zen Buddhist saying.

I wrote this book to help awaken some of my fellow Earth adventurers to some of the deeper mysteries of life. I would even go so far to say that, if you were given a choice of a million dollars or the information found in this book, you may be wise to take the book. I believe many of us are living day to day without some key knowledge we could benefit from, especially considering some of the things we humans are going through right now.

Early on, when in school, we start out learning to read and write so that we might thrive in this world and enjoy more of what it has to offer. Our parents and teachers share with us what they know, and much of it is helpful, and our education serves a purpose in preparing us for part of the life experience. After all, when one visits a new country, it helps to know the language and customs. For our own protection, we're told where the dangers lie so that we don't make a fatal misstep that causes our visit to this planet to be cut short. Without being told directly about forces like gravity, we are warned of its effects. There is plenty of time to learn the actual vocabulary and science later. Our first introduction to the fact that there might be some calamity associated with being human comes when we are learning to walk, and we fall. It can hurt.

Life here is relatively simple at first, and those who brought us here are charged with tending to our needs and watching over us. As time goes by we are left to fend for ourselves in a world that can be both hostile and welcoming at the same time. Those who came before us do their best to prepare

Introduction

us for what is to come but, in reality, they can only give us what they have learned themselves. We get their beliefs about how the world works as a template and map to start off with. However good the intentions behind our upbringing, we can still be sent out into the world with incomplete and often wrong information that can take a lifetime to unlearn. We are here only a short time, and my hope is that this book can assist you in wasting less of it.

I have been thinking for a number of years that we should be provided with a handbook for the experience of being human at an appropriate time after we arrive. I am not sure exactly when that time should be, but throughout history and in many cultures, there is some initiation or introduction to important knowledge that was given to members of the group, serving as a "rite of passage" that would allow young people to enter the next phase of their lives better prepared for what lay ahead. Perhaps the information in this book could serve a similar purpose.

In the meantime, regardless of how long we have been here or the number of years we have left, many of us might benefit from a better understanding of the underlying operating system and basic rules that encompass the Earth experience. As with gravity, an invisible force we all agree to be real, there are other forces and truths that are equally in play. It matters little if we believe in them or not, since the manifestation of their effects is real.

For those of you who read this book and have questions about the authenticity of the information provided, please know that this is both expected and welcomed. I hope the book stimulates inquiry and sends you on your own adventure and search. Most of us have time-tested belief systems in place, and I am not trying to convince anyone of anything. I am only sharing what I have learned in a simple and concise way to serve as an introduction to the basic principles for those who have come to this planet, for whatever reason.

It is an honor to be able to write this book and offer assistance to my fellow human beings who were brave enough to come to the planet for this magnificent adventure.

I had a life-altering experience in 1987 that psychologist Abraham Maslow might call a "peak experience." For spiritual folks, it could be called a "spiritual awakening." For a practicing Hindu, it would signify the opening of Kundalini. All I know is that, for me, the world was never to be quite the same afterward and it sent me on a thirty-year journey to try and understand it. I realize this gives me at least some verification that more exists beyond what we can see with our eyes. For many people, they have to reach this understanding without the benefit of direct experience. I feel I have an obligation to share what I've learned—the most important message being, *we are all connected.*

The question could be asked, why now? Why write a book thirty years into it? When this first happened to me, I wasn't aware that the information I received was accurate. I wanted to validate it in my own life and do my homework. It took a while, and I have found that the information I was given over those days and weeks was not something new or unique. This information has been available for thousands of years.

Even today, hundreds of books are sitting on bookshelves and authors and speakers are trying to reach us. I figured it was handled. After all, Oprah was on the case! Humanity was waking up, and maybe we would have a more enlightened world as a result. There are university programs studying the non-local nature of consciousness and science is uncovering new discoveries about a fully connected, interactive universe.

Over the past couple of years, I have felt that I should jump in and tell my story. I am not a writer by craft, but maybe my experiences and perspective might add something to the ongoing conversation.

This book is a fairly concise manual containing information about how to live effectively on the planet. When we arrive here, born on this plane, we get loaded up with lots of information, much of it non-essential to the things that matter most. Not the least of which are *who we are, why we are here, where do we go when we die?* And *what is our purpose?* What would happen if we had a curriculum in our schools that included the subject matter in this book?

What are the consequences to our belief systems of being fed from infancy onwards with erroneous information which is then constantly reinforced by the world around us?

Introduction

I have come to the conclusion that we already know what the real story is. All the information in this book is already in us, but we forget, suppress and resist.

This book may help you remember who you really are. Just as I woke up that day in 1987, today might just be your day. The world could use your assistance.

Chapter 1
We Are All Connected

When we try to pick anything out by itself, we find it's connected to everything else in the universe.

- John Muir

Throughout human history there has always been a person or group that tried to get us to understand that we are all one entity masquerading as being separate. This notion of non-duality, that we are not separate from the world we inhabit, is difficult to grasp. I dare say that, by the time we finish this chapter, you probably won't be any more convinced of the truth of this statement. We *feel* separate. Intellectually we may entertain the possibility that we are not separate, but it is what we actually *feel*—a feeling of separation—that becomes our experience of objective reality.

It turns out, we are both. Physicists now accept that the photons of a beam of light can present as both a wave and a particle when projected through a photosensitive device. When we dig into the operating system in quantum science, we find the counter-intuitive reality that the expectation of absolutes regarding quantum actions of sub-atomic particles has to be set aside. Those studying these effects have come to understand that the observer often unwittingly participates in the outcomes, making predictability elusive.

As an observer melds with the quantum action, they also become forever linked. The observer is not some scientist sitting in a lab, since consciousness itself is the observer. Nothing is outside of consciousness, as it is the animating force in everything in existence. As humans, we are aware of our own consciousness as it interacts with the world around us, and we are self-aware and engaged in our reality by being conscious of it. As an observer in the Earth experience, the world around us appears to be separate and distinct from us.

Science and mysticism have moved closer together. There is even an annual conference put on by the organization SAND, which stands for Science and Non-Duality. The event pairs up an unlikely combination of highly respected physicists from all over the world, together with spiritual thought leaders. The purpose is to share information and to coalesce the language around how to frame a common understanding of everything in our physical universe, everything on this planet, being linked through consciousness.

This is an astounding development when we stop to consider that our human consciousness is connected to every other person on Earth. It is as if we are all online with access to the Internet of knowledge. The practical benefit of this information is to bring scientists and mystics together toward a common goal. The objective they have in common through their respective disciplines is to enlighten us regarding the notion that we are all one.

One of the dominant theories that has come out of physics, and it has been around since early in the 20th Century, is something called *quantum entanglement*. One of the principles that comes out of this complex theory is the idea that particles that come into contact with or enter the orbit of each other, become mutually entangled to the extent that they begin to exhibit similar reactions.

Physicists have found that when two or more particles are linked in such a way, any change in one will simultaneously cause a change in the other, even if they are far apart, whether by thousands of miles or by thousands of light years. They essentially become one. Einstein found the whole idea a bit unsettling, calling this phenomenon "spooky action at a distance."

Previously experiments were limited to sub-atomic particles, but in 2015 they were able to achieve this with atoms, the building blocks of our physical reality. Using just a single photon to initiate the process, physicists from M.I.T. and the University of Belgrade report that they have successfully achieved mutual entanglement of a record number of atoms.

We Are All Connected

You may ask what the practical ramifications of this are, as it relates to the human experience? It would not take a huge leap forward in thinking to begin to assume that all of the atoms at some time were in contact with each other in the formation of the physical universe and of the planet we inhabit. Our physicality is made up of these atoms. This entanglement is permanent and it transcends distance.

Physicists are also learning that our very thoughts and emotions are made of electrical energy that can be captured to produce actions. Technology is on the verge of producing a reliable direct neural interface, or DNI programs, right now, allowing thoughts and impulses to create mechanical responses that will greatly benefit the disabled with physical implants called neuro-prosthetics.

Thoughts then enter the realm of potential entanglement. Remember that time and distance do not exist in the quantum world with regard to state. Non-locality describes the apparent ability of objects to instantaneously know about each other's state, even when separated by large distances, light-years apart.

Every energetic entity, including thoughts, exists in perpetuity. Within the theory of non-local entanglement, it could be argued that we live in a sea of others' thoughts and emotions and, on some level, we are impacted by them.

What physicists are beginning to understand is that everything is, at its core, vibrating energy, manifesting both as waves and as particles, intersecting with other waves and ultimately becoming entangled and consequently connected.

In the context of the human experience, all this is important information since the illusion presented within the space-time world is that everything is separate and distinct. Beyond that, there is a perceived hierarchy within society where some of those who are going through the human experience have more value than others. This means that certain people exist at the top of the pecking order, due to race, wealth, pedigree, nationality, or any variety of reasons we come up with for separating ourselves from others, in a never-ending cycle of seeking differentiation.

This is not a flaw in the human condition, since it happens as an integral element in the greater learning dynamic we agree to enter into as part of the Earth experience. It is part of the puzzle to be solved, the challenge to experience. Ultimately we must solve this puzzle both individually and for humanity as a whole. Again, this knowledge is not new, since we have been told this repeatedly, going back to Plato and Socrates. Now, however, it is being quantified and accepted by science. This validation allows for a much larger audience than ever before and it coincides with the unfolding that is happening on the planet right now. It appears we are ready.

Collective consciousness, the energy of thoughts and ideas of all the inhabitants that make up the ocean of humanity, reveals to us that something may be happening with regard to the health of the planet and that the *status quo* across the world is in flux. When we stop to consider that any pain, suffering or lack in the world is felt by every other inhabitant on some level, we are given the opportunity to address this on a large scale—to become conscious.

The collective consciousness of the planet is rising. It may appear otherwise, but that is part of the illusion of reality. As things change, there is a corresponding level of chaos that ensues. There is a saying, "the brighter the light, the darker the shadow." This is true for individuals as well as societies. History has shown that there are cycles and shifts. This includes civilizations that may have dominated former times and whose fortunes have reversed, in turn to become dominated themselves. Social upheaval has always been part of the human experience. These resulted from the natural flux in the overall learning environment on the planet.

The changes we are now experiencing—and they will become more profound—are arising from a humanity that is waking up. We are reaching a critical mass in a rising consciousness of vibrational energy, and there is nothing that can ultimately reverse the trend. It will probably be a bumpy ride since we are still operating out of the old paradigm of separateness. We humans tend to try all the options that don't work prior to reaching a breakthrough. Think of it as a massive remodeling job underway. If you have ever redone the kitchen in your home, you know that disruption of your daily life is part of that experience.

Someone who reads this book and finds that it resonates with them may be in the process of an awakening. There is so much information available about our true identity—who we really are—that it is a matter of not tripping over it as we blindly navigate our way through life, ignoring that which is in plain sight because our perceptual tools are attuned to the familiar. Our feeling and intuition may be telling us something that is in opposition to that which is perceived by our physical senses. In time, the default assumptions about our reality no longer satisfy. That is when we seek change.

Please know, however, that nothing we are personally doing is actually wrong. Remember, life is all about learning. We all get there in our own way, and everything works out as it should for the purpose of the human experience. Ultimately there is no judgement—that is a human invention.

Chapter 2
An Awakening Humanity

We cannot solve our problems with the same thinking we used when we created them.

~ Albert Einstein

If we understand and accept the science behind quantum entanglement and the connectedness of all life on this planet, we can start to appreciate the fact that the potential exists for us to be in communication with each other on some subtle level below the threshold of conscious awareness. What might be the ramifications of this? What if the overriding emotional state of the world impacts all of its inhabitants? Sensing the danger that precedes an earthquake or a weather anomaly, we know that animals and plants can have a reaction days or weeks ahead of such events.

There have been numerous experiments that show that what we feel and think impacts the life around us. One such experiment involved placing electrodes into yogurt cultures and having the experimenter think about negative events. The results showed that the culture reacted differently to those thoughts when compared with positive or neutral thoughts.

There have been numerous experiments involving plants and their ability to sense the intentions of their handlers. Just thinking about harming a plant will impact that plant's state, and a researcher can register this on a device that uses a similar technology to a polygraph to measure electrical activity. We know that plants communicate with other plants in their vicinity to let them know if there is a danger, where water can be found and to even assist others in their plant family. They may also communicate other information.

An Awakening Humanity

Birds in large flocks, such as starlings, can change direction instantaneously in a phenomenon called murmuration. The assumption at one time was that these animals must be reacting to some external provocation, but in studying large flocks by using slow motion video, they found this explanation to be insufficient. They have turned to the science of physics and how small particles know to react in coordinated fashion, to try to uncover the nature of this amazing display. There is some apparent networking in place in a starling murmuration that is not fully understood.

The physical and emotional connections that twins share have been studied, and a similar entanglement appears to exist between them. Comparable testing has been conducted using friends, acquaintances and family members. It has been found that if certain kinds of stimuli or stresses are introduced to one family member, it can register electrically in other close family members. Often this is proportional to the emotional closeness and attachment between the subjects. The interesting thing is that reactions occur instantaneously and without regard to the distance between them, not unlike what physicists understand about the quantum world and those connections.

What if it could be scientifically verified that there is something of a massive network that all humans are connected into? Such a research program, with the goal of verifying the reality of collective consciousness, is currently underway amongst a group of researchers in association with The Institute for Noetic Sciences. An excerpt from their website may be viewed at:

http://noosphere.princeton.edu/homepage4.html

The Global Consciousness Project, also called the EGG Project, is an international, multidisciplinary collaboration of scientists, engineers, artists and others. This organization collects data continuously from a global network of physical random number generators located in sixty-five host sites around the world. The archive contains more than twelve years of random data in parallel sequences of synchronized 200-bit trials every second.

"Our purpose is to examine subtle correlations that may reflect the presence and activity of consciousness in the world.

We predict structure in what should be random data, associated with major global events. When millions of us share intentions and emotions, the GCP/EGG network data show meaningful departures from expectation and has billion to one odds against chance. This is a powerful finding based in solid science."

Practical Applications of Unified Consciousness

If we were to randomly poll large numbers of people on their general feelings of comfort, satisfaction and wellbeing, what do you think the results might be?

It seems that we are under a constant barrage of information. Much of it comes from news sources that consider their mission to keep us continually titillated and engaged. If we tune to a cable news program and watch it for thirty minutes, we are likely to see graphic film footage of some pretty bad things. No wonder that we may want to take a break, go watch a pussycat video on the computer or one of a puppy playing the piano, every once in a while. There is no apparent conspiracy surrounding the reasons why we are so inundated with information. It is simply a matter of the presence of commerce and the need for us to be attentive to the messages of those advertisers who sponsor those sources of the news and information.

News outlets understand that they are competing for our attention, and our primary importance lies in the fact that we are potential consumers and they are obligated to deliver us to their sponsors. Over time the public becomes desensitized, and it requires vigilance to stay ahead of what might hold our attention. Our tastes change rapidly, and interest trends can turn on a dime.

While we may be distracted with news of plane crashes in Indonesia or some celebrity who entered rehab, there is a real calamity in the making that is not getting the attention it deserves in the press—the effects of climate change and the potential consequences of inaction to address it for all life on the planet. Some of this goes back to our status as the consumer and the concern that people may be less likely to go out and buy a new car if they think they might not be around to enjoy it. Who cares about good cell phone coverage when there may not be enough water to drink? There are certain news stories that are inconvenient because they may dampen the urge to purchase. It's not like we don't recognize that it is going on: we tolerate it because there is a payoff to not having to face the hard facts in what amounts to systemic denial.

Our nervous systems are hardwired to react to any perceived danger. When there is news of a terror attack somewhere in the world, unconsciously we may respond to it as a threat to our individual safety, even though it is on the other side of the world. The closer the proximity or relevancy, the higher the anxiety. There was a time when we knew only what was going on in our own village, but now we can be aware of what is going on in villages all over the world, almost the instant something happens.

Those who treat health issues understand the physical and psychological consequences of prolonged arousal that continually engages our flight-or-fight response. Chronic low-grade stress is affecting us below the threshold of awareness, and it slowly sucks the life out of our health. The purpose of pointing this out is that, over time, this scenario will ultimately take a toll on the collective human psyche.

Earth is currently populated by more than eight billion people who, at some point in the not too distant future, will be aware that they are competing for dwindling resources on a planet that is overheating and may very likely run out of water. No need to sugar-coat it, this is going to be our new reality. At no time in the history of humankind has there been the real possibility of mass extinction. So, it is understandable that we might not be taking seriously the possibility of this happening.

The rate of change in our biosphere is rapidly accelerating and, because the extinction of any species can potentially lead to the extinction of others that are bound to that species in this interdependent web of life, the numbers of subsequent extinctions are likely to snowball in the coming years, as all ecosystems will be impacted. We humans are part of that ecosystem.

The only time there was a comparably massive die-off was 65 million years ago, wiping out the dinosaurs and 90% of all other life on the planet. We were not around for that, but this time we are, and the irony is that, this time, we are the main contributing factor—not active volcanoes or a meteor hitting the Earth. We are now in a situation where we need to figure out how we as a species are going to deal with this.

The first step toward this is mass acknowledgment that this predicament exists. This has been difficult to achieve since there is little acknowledgment of the urgency of the situation from those who control the megaphone. Meanwhile the majority of climate scientists, some world governments, the United Nations, NASA and the Pentagon agree that we are in uncharted waters with regard to the nature of what is a legitimate crisis.

The argument has been effectively muted by confusion that is being perpetrated by parties who feel that their interests would not benefit from the necessary actions it would take to curtail the effects of climate change. They have convinced enough people through disinformation campaigns that there is no proof that the Earth is warming or, if it is, man has nothing to do with its causation, and therefore can't produce a remedy that is less disruptive and costly than the problem itself.

The time we have taken in debating the issue could have been used to stop the progression, or at least to slow it down. Those who took us into the Iraq war rationalized that, if there was even a 1% chance that Saddam Hussein was working on a nuclear program, then it was reason enough to proceed—that's according to *New York Times* writer, Ron Suskind, in his best-selling book *The One Percent Doctrine*.

The certainty level met this threshold back in 1988, when a NASA scientist, James Hansen, warned congress in a hearing before the Energy and Natural Resources Committee that the Earth was heating up due to the greenhouse effect and it could be bad news for humanity. Widespread attention was again focused on the issue in 2006, when the movie *An Inconvenient Truth* was released, focusing on the scientific basis for concern about climate change.

The film received considerable attention and ultimately won an Oscar for best documentary for that year. Al Gore, who shared a Nobel Prize with the Intergovernmental Panel on Climate Change (IPCC) for their contribution to the topic, was behind the movie and starred in it. In the summer of 2017, he followed up with a second film, *An Inconvenient Sequel—Truth to Power*. In it, he admits that he underestimated in 1997 how quickly the repercussions of human-assisted climate change would progress. In the meantime, President Trump pulled us out of the Paris Climate Agreement and put a climate change denier in charge of the EPA—the very agency that was created to help protect Americans from corporate assaults on the environment that can adversely affect our lives.

Getting legislation to match the urgency of the situation has been made all the more difficult with Supreme Court decisions that have allowed corporations to donate unlimited contributions to politicians. The richest companies in the world are fossil fuel companies. According to watchdog groups that track corporate financial influence in Congress, there are 679 lobbyists working for the oil and gas industry in Washington DC. Over 400 of them were former elected or appointed government officials. These statistics came from the Senate Office of Public Records. For more information on this, you can go directly to the page on the *Open Secrets* website that addresses contributions made by this sector to those who are elected to look out for the public's best interest.

https://www.opensecrets.org/industries/indus.php?ind=E01

In 2015 in the documentary *The Merchants of Doubt,* based on a book by the same name, we learned of the methodology used to confuse the public and taint the data on the topic of climate change. According to researchers and interviews with insiders, the fossil fuel industry followed the example of a tobacco industry disinformation campaign that involved successfully skewing public understanding of the health consequences of smoking, and they applied it to climate change. They have continued to use that playbook in an effort to buy time.

Public relations firms advised the tobacco industry not to deny that tobacco could cause cancer. They were instead advised to create doubt. Doubt became their product. In the film, there was compelling video of the talking points used, saying that there was no substantiating evidence that linked smoking to cancer. Evidence did exist, however, and it was first uncovered by the tobacco industry itself.

When whistleblowers made this known, the lawsuits began but, by that time, hundreds of billions of dollars in profits had already been realized. According to the book, the inevitable lawsuits and compensatory losses were apparently baked into the cake. The same scenario is happening again with climate change. It could be reasonably assumed that each additional day that confusion can be sustained, is another day of profit before the inevitable regulations—and public ire—are set in motion.

We are, to some extent, responsible accessories to this charade. It is understandable that we might find comfort in the notion that climate change could just be a hyped controversy. Or, if it isn't, that we can't do anything about it. To assimilate something of this magnitude and scale is difficult.

The most recent Intergovernmental Panel on Climate Change (IPCC) report, issued in 2014 by the World Meteorological Organization (WMO) and the United Nations, stated that sea levels are rising 60% faster than predicted in the 2007 IPCC report and warming has accelerated much faster than past models predicted. In other words, because scientists tend to be conservative in their estimates, the reality is more urgent than is being reported.

One of the main purposes of this book is to open minds to the potential of using the knowledge that we are all connected, and that what happens to some of us can affect all of us. This is best accomplished if we understand more fully where we currently are in relation to the mission we each might have, or the purpose we want to explore. Our individual consciousness and subsequent goals for our lives are inextricably linked to those of others. The more we know, the more likely we are to make an informed decision.

We can have differing opinions on a variety of matters, but I suspect that I am stepping out on a pretty sturdy limb to suggest that preservation of life on the planet for future generations might be something we all want. This transcends ideological affiliations and it includes all groups. If there is doubt, then perhaps we should assume the premise behind the "one percent doctrine", as it might apply to climate change. Even the most skeptical of observers might be able to acknowledge that we have exceeded that low threshold for taking some action. Nothing that we have ever faced on this planet in human history would justify an understanding that we are all in this together more than the reality of climate change. A remark Ronald Reagan made before the United Nations in 1987 is somewhat prescient:

An Awakening Humanity

"Perhaps we need some outside universal threat to make us recognize this common bond. I occasionally think how quickly our differences worldwide would vanish if we were facing an alien threat from outside this world."

Humanity faces something that equals this right now, and with it comes an opportunity to recognize that the solution will only be found in our ability to cooperate with each other. In our present state of evolutionary consciousness, it remains an open question as to how long that might take to be realized. We don't have decades to figure this out, much less millennia. It will take, as Einstein suggested, a different way of thinking to solve this.

Currently, a massive influx of thought energy is moving us toward a shift. Human consciousness is aware, on a primal level, that something is not right. Much of the chaos in the world can be attributed to the uneasy feeling that a dramatic change is underway, in much the same way that animals react preceding an earthquake.

This energy is being provided by people who have a raised consciousness. In many instances, this has come about voluntarily amongst those who have an interest in the pursuit of activities such as meditation, yoga and other such disciplines that require the practitioner to step outside ordinary awareness. Others are thrust less willingly into a new and often permanent, paradigm for understanding the nature of our reality, and of near-death and other non-local experiences. There are many ways that consciousness becomes raised. The amazing thing is that the world doesn't need everyone to participate for the whole of human consciousness on the planet to be affected. Only a certain number of people are required to reach what we call critical mass.

Critical mass can occur when enough parts of a whole reach a certain level. This subsequently initiates a chain reaction in which all the other parts are automatically raised to that level as well. A good example is seen when we heat water. There comes a point where enough molecules reach boiling temperature, and this elicits a chain reaction so that all the remaining molecules are raised to that temperature and the water reaches a full boil. To reach a critical mass in consciousness, enough individuals need to reach a certain level of consciousness. A chain reaction will occur, bringing the rest of humanity up to that level as well. The good news is that all that is really needed now is for those who have awakened to take action.

We can take some comfort in the fact that there are many who believe that we have enough to do this right now. It is estimated that 4% of the world's population has had what we might define as "mystical" experiences, that have provided them with a better understanding of the true nature of reality and a greater sense of empathy for others, an elevated ability to love and practice acceptance. Combine these people with those who have volunteered to adopt states of mind that allow for a shift away from the egocentric, with a desire to be of service to their fellow humans, and we may very well have the numbers necessary to elevate consciousness across the planet.

This elevation doesn't resolve the issue—it only creates a climate more beneficial to a desired outcome. Remember that consciousness is a vibration of energy. As the waves of this energy intercept other lower waves, it is not unlike what happens with the wakes of boats when they cross each other's paths in the ocean—there is some violence in the collision of the wakes but, ultimately, they settle back into the body of water. As the waves of higher vibratory energy raise the overall energy on the planet and exponentially affect all its inhabitants, the climate for cooperation is increased.

That is about the best we can hope for since there is no scenario where it includes all. We do need enough world citizens and sufficient leadership to make the shift. As we have seen in the past, a relatively small number with the courage to light the fire that produces the energy to initiate significant change is often all that is required. There are many examples of this throughout history but, just in our lifetime, we have witnessed social change on a grand scale catalyzed by people like Martin Luther King, Rosa Parks and Gandhi.

As we have learned from history, changes in attitude do not come without significant action and effort, and the buy-in of the power structure, at some point, is critical. Major countries and multinational corporations are needed as signatories to the kinds of agreements and legislation that will sanction and anchor the real changes that are necessary to promote cooperative change. This does not require an altruistic rationale on their part, and it doesn't really matter if the motivation is self-serving for economic or political reasons.

Humanity is faced with some hard choices. As individuals, we hold the power to act, and that action will register toward the totality of change. To sit and do nothing is an option as well. As for me, I wanted to contribute what I could, and so I wrote this book with the intent of helping to wake up more of my fellow human beings. As for the environment, I started the Green Energy Project...

www.greenenergyproject.earth

...with the goal of helping to mobilize individuals to make changes in their lifestyle, their home and community in order to benefit the environment.

As always, it is up to us to uncover what our unique contribution might be. All of us possess great gifts and talents, should we choose to mobilize them. If you are so inclined, now might be a good time to do so.

Chapter 3

Spooky Science

Science Searches for Answers

Early on we didn't have much to go on in our attempts to explain the inner workings of the world around us. For all we knew, the world was governed by supernatural forces beyond our control. Outside forces interceded in all aspects of our experiential world. If the rains didn't come or an earthquake shook the ground, then it was attributed to the capriciousness of gods who were ignoring our plight or unhappy with our actions, resulting in punishment. We imbued these gods with characteristics, emotions and a rationale we could identify with. In an attempt to head off any future calamities, strategies were sought that might placate them. In an effort to demonstrate respect, edifices were constructed and rituals were established to please them.

Differing opinions about what the gods wanted ultimately led to the formation of religions to accommodate particular notions of the perceived preferences of the gods. Apparently, they were a very particular lot when it came to how they were to be worshiped, and we needed to understand what they wanted—because the next drought, flood or earthquake was always right around the corner. This naturally led to the establishment of deterrents in the form of laws and punishments for those who didn't adhere to the designated rituals. One of the things we knew for sure: the gods didn't like to have too many questions asked. Challenges to their authority were quickly dealt with, so as not to upset them and bring this whole thing crashing down on our collective heads.

Troublemakers did show up—intellectually curious individuals who knew that there must be more to their world than the answers they were getting, daring to ask the big questions. Today we call them scientists. They thought it was worth risking reputation, personal freedom, and possibly their lives, in their pursuit of the knowledge that would make sense of the world around them.

One such radical was Polish born Nicolaus Copernicus who lived in the 16th Century. He had the audacity to advance the theory, in his book *On the Revolutions of the Celestial Spheres*, that the Sun—not the Earth—was the center of our solar system. In fear of retribution, he made sure not to authorize its release until he lay on his deathbed. He fully understood the times he was in and what repercussions awaited him upon publication.

In the following century, Galileo Galilei was among those who fully accepted and advanced this cosmological reordering of the planets, as suggested by Copernicus. The Catholic Church, under Pope Urban VIII, held that it was heresy and Galileo was arrested. Any notion of a contrary explanation was considered blasphemy and punishable by death. Galileo ended up having to bargain for his life by agreeing to renounce his scientific beliefs and he spent the remainder of his life under house arrest. It took some 300 years for the Church to admit that Galileo was right, and finally to clear his name.

The general notion that the Earth was at the center of the universe persisted long after science had proven it wrong. Consider also that a substantial number of people could not accept that the world was spherical and not a flat surface, as our senses suggested. A group calling themselves the Flat Earth Society persists even today. Old beliefs die hard.

Every time we think we have closed the case on a comfortable understanding about how our world works, it gets nudged out of the way by new information. In the 19th Century science was so certain of the infallibility of Newton's conclusions that it was declared by scientists of the day that there was no need for further exploration. Newton and his predecessors had arrived at the best conclusions available to them at the time. His explanations about the mechanics of our universe were the accepted model of physical reality for over 200 years, remaining unchallenged until Albert Einstein released his paper on general relativity in 1905.

Einstein's calculations refuted the long-accepted notion that gravity was not a magnetic force as Newton claimed, but instead an interaction between the fabric of space and mass.

He put forward a radical theory that space and time were, in fact, one seamless phenomenon. Einstein's discoveries involving the interactive relationship between space, time and matter were so challenging that, like those before him, he was accused of heresy, this time *within* the scientific establishment. All Einstein did, as all the other scientists before him had done, was to take the ball he was handed and move it down the field.

Both Newton and Einstein worked primarily within the parameters of the observable world. Special Relativity was focused on the study of forces that influenced the behavior of large objects. In the 1920s a parallel branch of physics erupted, focusing on the tiny world that made up the infrastructure of our physical universe—molecules and atoms. The expectation was scientists would find properties and actions that mirrored the visible world in miniature. Instead, what they found was so unexpected that it turned the whole world of physics upside down and shook it up. The result was a monumental shift in our understanding of the nature of physical reality. In the atomic and subatomic world, very strange things happened that contradicted everything we thought we understood about our universe. Certainty and predictability went out of the window, only to be replaced with randomness and unpredictability.

One of the sacred tenets of science was always the predictability of phenomena. Einstein famously said, "God doesn't play dice," referring to the actions governing the universe.

Quantum theory proved otherwise. For one thing, in the quantum world, one could only narrow down theories to the *probabilities* of certain outcomes. When Einstein referred to quantum physics as a spooky science, he was specifically addressing what later was to be called *quantum entanglement*—attributed primarily to his contemporary, physicist Niels Bohr. Although they admired each other's work, they had a very public dispute about his theories that persisted through the remainder of Einstein's life. Just as Einstein challenged Newton, quantum theory undermined the accepted science of that time. So, it goes—on and on.

By now we should have a better understanding of the limits of what we are likely to know. As with a Russian doll, we open one up only to find another smaller version inside. Again and again, we overestimate our human intellectual capacity to penetrate the unknown and arrive at explanations that will withstand the test of time. Uncertainty and paradox are not the scientist's friend.

It may turn out that the science fiction written today, providing provocative insights for movies such as *The Matrix*, *Sliding Doors*, *Avatar* and *Inception*, will find their place alongside the realities that have come to fruition in the works of Huxley, Orwell, Philip K. Dick and Asimov.

One of the repercussions of the uncertain nature of reality is that there is now more freedom than before to go outside the previously rigid lines of mainstream scientific inquiry, even into what some might call "kooky science." If a scientist can produce a calculation that says the world might be a virtual reality simulation, not unlike a video game, instead of being shunned they might find themselves invited to speak in front of prestigious scientific forums and have their work published in mainstream journals. Take as an example, Dr. S. James Gates, Jr., a highly respected theoretical physicist and Professor of Physics at the University of Maryland, who has gained considerable attention for his discovery that, within quantum mathematics, there seems to be evidence of a binary error-correcting block code, eerily similar to that found in the programming code for video games and search engines like Google.

Serious discussions are taking place within the scientific community that what we think of as reality might be a holographic, multidimensional computer program, not unlike a virtual reality video game. We are both operator and participant in the game, making choices about which doors to open, routes to take, and how the story ultimately is to advance. If that isn't enough, there may be unlimited versions of us all playing a game and making different choices. Think of an infinite number of games of chess going on simultaneously with every possible move being played out. Maybe we are playing against ourselves from the future, just to make it more interesting. Chew on that for a while.

Our egos will most likely rebel against the notion that there might be many versions of us running around in other universes doing Lord-knows-what. Human beings are generally linear thinkers with a fixed reality, with sequential time separating the past, present and future and defining the way in which we experience the world. Our senses validate this for us every minute of the day. We are not unlike those who demanded that the world was flat, and did so based on the limited amount of information they had available through their senses and validated by a consensus world view. Contrary to our experience, however, science has proven that in the substructure of our reality, time, as we experience it here in our earthly playpen, doesn't exist. It turns out that all time is simultaneous. Just as the mystics have told us for eons, there is only the Now.

The Quantum Universe

I would like to attempt to align some of the concepts I've presented with the goal of bringing in some scientific perspective that can help validate some of the more outrageous ideas that have been described. Hopefully, it will bring some context for a better understanding of the fact that there is much more to the reality we think we know.

I can understand how it might be difficult to wrap your mind around the ideas here. Even scientists are in a quandary about things they are learning about the universe. Particle physicists are having to subscribe to ways of thinking that are associated more with mystics.

The thirst to learn and evolve our understanding of how things work appears to be hardwired into our DNA. If you watch a child playing with a toy, it's not surprising to see the child take it apart at some point. I remember cutting open golf balls to see what was inside. That is what we humans do: we try to solve the mystery of what lies within.

Throughout history, humankind has attempted to explain the natural world within the context of knowledge possessed at any given time. Although scientific materialism still dominates all explanations of how the universe works, we continue to unveil such astounding discoveries that scientists from the most prestigious institutions in the world don't understand the inner workings of our universe with any degree of certainty.

The early 20th Century saw the birth of modern science, first with Einstein and his Theory of Relativity, regarding the interaction of large objects, such as planets. At the same time, a new science sought to explain the smallest interactions within the world of atoms—*quantum mechanics.*

Both shook up the scientific community of its day, but it was quantum theory that really started the fire of controversy. With each new discovery within the tiny world of atoms, it just keeps getting weirder.

You might want to become familiar with these terms as they relate to the quantum world:

Particle: referring to the small bits called atoms, and the subatomic particles that are found in and around them, making up the invisible world that is the foundation of matter and energy. It includes things like electrons, protons, neutrons, photons, quarks, pions, muons, kaons, neutrinos and bosons.

Uncertainty Principle (Heisenberg's Uncertainty Principle): in the subatomic world, it is not possible to predict the actions of particles with any certainty, regarding momentum and position. This is an example of the random nature of this reality.

Measurement Problem: for physicists this is the most confounding characteristic of the quantum world. Particles do not seem to exist until they are measured—that is, observed. The universe is essentially just energy waves of probability until it is observed.

Quantum Entanglement: whenever two particles interact with each other in any way they are forever connected, and whatever one particle experiences, it instantaneously impacts on the other one regardless of the distance between them.

String Theory: the theory that everything in the universe is made up of invisible vibrating strings of energy existing simultaneously in multiple universes. They are imperceptible to us from our vantage point in a three-dimensional universe.

Many Worlds Theory: this theory states that every variation of a potential state breaks off into a separate universe or, in our case, a separate world where a version of us exists for every choice we make.

Here are some of the weird and strange reasons why quantum physics might be called *spooky*: a particle such as an electron can be in two places at once and it can be in more than one state, as either a wave of energy or as a particle. This is called superposition.

- Particles can be both a wave and a particle simultaneously;
- Particles act differently or change state when they are observed or measured;
- Particles can pop into existence out of nowhere and then disappear;
- Atoms are 99.9999% empty space. If you removed all the space from all the atoms that make up the human race, the amount of matter would be about the size of a sugar cube.

If two particles interact with each other, they become entangled in such a way that what happens to one particle will instantaneously happen to the other, even if they are on opposite sides of the universe.

What do we really understand about our universe? Well, as it turns out, not a lot, at least not with any real certainty. We have placeholder theories that are really just pieces of a giant puzzle to be searched for on a table that stretches to infinity.

What we do know about accounts for only 4% of all the matter in the universe. The remaining 96% may consist of something called dark matter and dark energy. Scientists know very little about them and have no proof of their existence, other than that astronomers have seen some effect of a gravitational force being excreted from light out in the cosmos, with no corresponding celestial body around it.

Ultimately, the more we know, the more questions arise. We are not unlike a paramecium trying to make sense of the water drop it inhabits. For all it knows, that drop is the whole universe, and nothing else exists beyond it.

Chapter 4

Big Questions

Behind every problem there's a question trying to ask itself. Behind every question there's an answer trying to reveal itself. Behind every answer there's an action trying to take place. Behind every action there's a way of life trying to be born.

~ Michael Beckwith

Where do I come from? Why am I here? Where do I go when I die?

These are big questions we all ask at some point in our lives. This book is primarily about self-discovery, of the kind that comes once someone starts looking for answers to these larger questions. There is some energy contained in asking them, and they can trigger a reaction from the universe in response. When sincerely invoked, the results can vary. It might be a gentle push, with a comfortable ride to the finish, or it may open a doorway to a wild adventure that at times will shake up your life. It is just like the Rolling Stones song that says: "*You can't always get what you want, but if you try sometimes, you just might find, you get what you need.*"

Children may ask where they come from and they are provided with a biology-based response from their parents. It could be that the question is not fully understood. Children may be asking something more profound, and we aren't prepared to answer because we have not dipped deeper into such things ourselves.

As adults, we become entranced with the cultural constructs we live within, and often we define ourselves within the boundaries of what we do for a living, where we reside, and our family origins—our social standing can denote our value and identity on Earth. We further define ourselves by ethnicity, gender and group affiliations—such as our religion. These are answers we give when asked who we are.

For much of our lives, we are busy establishing ourselves within the fabric of society and evaluating our status on a basis of comparison with others. This is currently the dominant state of mind for much of humanity. This is understandable since just maintaining the basic necessities of life—food, shelter, work, and family—can take up much of a person's time and energy.

American Psychologist Abraham Maslow described a hierarchy of needs that must be fulfilled for many to be able to free the mind to higher brain function, to allow for what he called self-actualization. In this state, an individual engages a higher part of the brain, the neocortex—the most recent evolutionary addition to the cerebral cortex. It is the part of the brain that questions and seeks to understand the world outside of its immediate physical environment. Though we all have moments of enlightenment, for much of humanity it is the lower brain function that dominates our actions and controls our world view. Within the limbic brain, and particularly the amygdala, are physiological remnants of our ancient ancestors' essential survival mechanisms.

These structures, also referred to as the reptilian brain, served us well, it seems—evidenced by the fact that we are still here. The dominance of the lower brain, however, is what causes us to group into tribes for greater safety, for fear of those who are different from us, and to some extent to keep us captive to our fearful emotions. The dramatic rise of health issues due to stress are primarily a result of our over-reaction to perceived threats in the world. The media, and people who seek power, understand how to reach our reptilian brain, and how to use that knowledge to influence our decision-making. When it comes to a choice between our need for safety and anything else, it's no contest—safety usually wins.

Much of humanity seems to be stuck in survival mode or it rests in a state of complacency. The impetus to interrupt the *status quo* is generally lacking. Things may not be great, but they are good enough. One of the incentives for a more evolved form of thinking may come out of necessity. Many species on the planet are under threat of extinction, and it could include us humans at some point if we don't take action.

Scientists agree with 98% certainty that climate change is real and is caused by human activities on this planet. There is good evidence that, if we don't act with a keen sense of urgency, an uncertain outcome for all of Earth's inhabitants is likely. Lower brain thinking is not going to get us out of this predicament. It will take the loftier processing of the neocortex to promote states of cooperation and empathy that might effect change. People of disparate cultural groups, even those who don't consider one another to be allies, will be required to work together to resolve this challenge.

The selflessness that defines a state of self-actualization, such as being able to think compassionately of the plight of others, will allow for the type of cooperative response that can result in positive change. It may be possible that feeling the emotional rewards of such actions can open up a path for mass advancement to an even more expansive stage of evolutionary thinking—self-transcendence. This state is defined by spiritual ideas, such as considering oneself an integral part of the universe, or that we are all connected and that what happens to any one of us affects everyone and everything else.

Chapter 5
Our Search for Answers

When we come to the planet we are not given a handbook on how to navigate effectively through earthly experience. That is one of the purposes of this book, to help you who have chosen the Earth experience to understand the rules of the game. Part of the adventure is to figure it out. Like any good mystery or adventure novel, clues are presented along the way to find the treasure or solve the mystery. The treasure map is parsed out, and the clues come in the form of symbols in our dreams, or events ripe with meaning, and it often comes from other actors in our life-story.

The amnesia that prevents us from remembering who we are also comes into play when it comes to figuring out how to navigate through the world, discovering all of our abilities. We are all provided a toolbox with exactly what we need for our life journey, no matter how it might appear. No one is at a disadvantage when it comes to accomplishing the mission and living out the story. What might appear to be an advantage or a liability, due to physical attributes, social rank, race, illness, disability or wealth are all illusory when it comes to what we actually came here to experience and learn.

We all have the instructions. It is just that they are purposely hidden in the least obvious place—inside of us. Everything is right there, waiting for us to unlock it with the knowledge that is contained within the deeper mind, the part of us that connects with all knowledge, hiding in plain sight. It is also coded in our cells and programmed into our DNA. The keys can be discovered as we learn to love, find compassion for those who need it most, cross a threshold, take bold action toward our purpose and face our fears.

When we start to ask big questions, whether consciously or unconsciously, we are actually asking to begin the process of remembering where we hid the keys. To the degree

Our Search for Answers

that we are earnest in our search for answers and the intention behind them, we learn where they are. This is the essence of the process of waking up to our potential of who we really are, behind the facade. Becoming conscious of this allows us to utilize that knowledge to fulfill our selected purpose. Much of what we think we are learning anew is actually recollection. When we ask questions, answers are provided—always. We may not recognize the response because they do not come in the manner we expect, or they are subtle. It could also be that we are not ready to accept the answers that come.

Our timing for asking the big questions is an individual matter. It could be that we set the alarm clock for a wake-up call. I think this is what happened to me, because there really wasn't anything else going on in my life that might have precipitated the dramatic shift I experienced. For some, the search is for a better understanding of the life circumstances that have shaken up their world, and they find themselves asking, "*Why me?*". What has worked in the past may no longer be effective. For others, they may have achieved everything they thought they needed to be happy and fulfilled and, for some reason, they don't feel fulfilled.

Becoming dissatisfied with our lives, experiencing outcomes we neither wanted nor anticipated, even suffering from anxiety and depression, can be considered gifts if those circumstances let us know that we are off course in our mission, or not using the wonderful tools we brought with us. If you want to know what your purpose is, look at what you are most interested in—your passions. What work would you do for free? What injustices would you like to fix if you could?

What you can do at any moment, to better understand where you are in the process, is to look around you. Are you in a place you want to be? Are you doing an activity that you feel energized by?

In the bigger picture of the reality you have created, do you generally feel enthusiastic, or are most days a slog, when you can't wait for the day to end so you can go to sleep? Are the people you're surrounded with in your daily routine positive and happy, and do they possess integrity?

Are the traits of curiosity and creativity that you had as a child still active, or have they been relegated, deemed nonessential? How's your physical health? Do you have the energy to do the things you enjoy doing? Are depression and anxiety your predominant moods?

As you answer these questions, you may notice that you begin thinking in a more expansive way. How does that feel? When we think reflectively, we rationalize those answers that will help us avoid cognitive dissonance—it comes when we are presented with information that runs counter to the narrative surrounding the reality we have created. As they are pondered, the emotions that arise about these questions contain valuable information. It is in *feeling* that we are guided. We can trick our own minds, but feelings always tell the truth—they nudge us to stay on track.

When we make the decision to acquiesce to a deeper calling and to consciously enter the journey, there is an immediate response from the universe. By making this choice, to be willing to start the journey, we are joined by forces waiting to assist us. There can be an energetic rush as the winds that have been building up to fill our sails gain momentum. This can be disconcerting because it can involve the current life being dismantled and new elements may not yet be apparent.

It takes courage to go through this period, and some trust is needed. What may not be apparent is that help is always there. We are always supported and comforted during this time. It comes almost as if the deeper part of who we are has been waiting for us to make a choice. Unsolicited outside help has always been there as well, but this assistance is different. It is there to help us fulfill the master script and reach great heights, if that is our desire.

If expertise needs to be engaged, specialists can be called in to assist. Getting help with a project from supernatural resources is not a new concept. Throughout history, artists believed in the existence of "muses" which could be called upon to assist with insights and inspiration from beyond this world. This is not to suggest that help is limited to creative people who have crossed over.

We do need to develop the required skills to be able to bring a creation into this world. If we don't possess the skills, but the desire for something is strong enough, we might obtain them through study and effort, so that we can begin to make our ideas tangible. Michelangelo is noted to have said, regarding his sculptures—and I paraphrase—the image already exists in a block of granite, and his task was to free it. Mozart awoke with full symphonies in his head and wrote his first one at the age of five.

In 2004 the television news show *60 Minutes* ran a piece on a musical prodigy who was twelve at the time, attending Julliard School of Music. This young composer had already written five symphonies—some had been performed by major orchestras. When asked by the show's interviewer how he came up with these pieces, he said he didn't know, that they just show up in his head fully composed, and he just writes them down as if he is listening to a full orchestra in his mind.

There are many stories of well-known inventions where ideas and ways to build them come in dreams. These opportunities to create come to those who have put in the effort to learn the skills of their craft. The hard work of becoming proficient in something allows for a collaboration that can bring about genius.

Chapter 6
Where Do I Come From?

You are an eternal, restless energy in search of experience. The animating force that you identify with has always been and it will always be. Coming to this planet and understanding what it is like to be a human being is one of the key kinds of experience available to you. Earth is not your permanent home—it is analogous to going away to school or taking a trip. When you travel, you probably have a plan, make temporary living arrangements with the understanding that you will return home at some point, bringing with you the things you have learned, people you met and events that will be retained.

This is part of the totality of a new version of you that evolves out of what has been experienced on the journey. It is a temporary excursion, the purpose being learning, and that may include selected side-trips and contingencies that can be found in any travel itinerary. You are much more a tourist than a resident.

Some people like to plan their trips with all the stops, sites, meals, events, classes and circumstances laid out in detail, while others may want to just jump on a plane and see what happens when they arrive at their destination. The same is true for those who opt into the human adventure. The choice can be made in advance to specialize in a particular area of study or attention, mastering a particular knowledge or skill. Just as likely as it could be for fun and for the excitement of the adventure.

There are many reasons why someone may choose to visit Earth to participate in the human experience. You may or may not have a sense of what that is. The simple act of asking is often enough to have that mystery begin to reveal itself. It may not come in the way you might expect, however. Some know from a very young age why they exist. These are generally the ones that have planned their trip in detail. There is no single way of experiencing life here, and one way is not necessarily more valuable than another. We all ultimately get something important we can use, to be added to the whole of who we are.

Why choose the Earth experience? I don't know if this is unique to this planet, but my sense is that it has something to do with our not fully remembering *who we really are.* Coming into the human experience involves our taking on a particular persona and role that fits what we came here to learn and accomplish. This amnesia appears to be an essential condition, allowing us to become more fully immersed in the human experience. Not remembering is by design.

We are not unlike actors who are able to completely inhabit a role, yet we can forget that we are actually playing a role. We become convinced that we are the character we are playing, with little recollection of the original self that set it all up. There's a line from Shakespeare's play *As You Like It*:

"All the world's a stage, and all the men and women merely players; they have their exits and their entrances, and one man in his time plays many parts."

This resonates even with those who might have little interest in Shakespeare and his wealth of work. It could be that we relate on some level to the truth it contains. It is not unusual to find reminders of our true nature in the arts and even current popular culture.

There are many examples throughout literature from sources all over the globe: Homer, Shakespeare, Cervantes, Keats, Thoreau and Whitman are examples, and their works have stood the test of time, universally celebrated for the wisdom they imparted over many generations. This is in part due to the underlying truth they contain, which speaks to our authentic nature. In my lifetime, there have been examples of books that found exceptionally large audiences. Many of the best-selling books of the 20th Century may owe their popularity to the clues they provided about who we are and about the shared human experience. Books such as Kahlil Gibran's *The Prophet*, Richard Bach's *Jonathan Livingston Seagull*, Paulo Coelho's *The Alchemist*, James Redfield's *The Celestine Prophecy*, Gary Zukav's *Seat of the Soul*, Don Miguel Ruiz's *The Four Agreements* and Rhonda Byrne's *The Secret*, hit a collective chord within the psyche of millions of people.

Every day we encounter reminders and opportunities to remember that, if only we are open to the idea, we are actually much more than we think we are. The itinerary for discovery of our deeper natures is often found within our DNA, the map we bring into each lifetime.

City of Acrobats
Drawing reproduced from *The Story of Life* by Luigi and Kate Agnelli

In a world where danger and fear is everywhere, there exists a city where you can still live in joy and happiness… it's the city of the acrobats! But if you look carefully in the lower left corner, you will see a girl holding onto a rope… if she lets go, everyone will fall. The significance of this is that we must be together to be happy. A happy man alone in this life is never a truly happy man!

Chapter 7
Rules of the Game

Life is the only game in which the object of the game is to learn the rules.

~ Ashleigh Brilliant, Author/Cartoonist

As stated previously, when we first come into the Earth experience we are dependent on others to take care of our basic needs. They do the planning and caretaking, educating us as best they can about how the world works from their understanding and perspective. We don't have our own beliefs established yet, so we may adopt their world view for a while. As we have more exposure to others and to wider sources of information, we begin to build on that foundation to form our own unique ideas and perceptions.

We are introduced to institutions provided by the community, outside of our home and family, where the base of our knowledge is expanded even more, and our reality gets further defined. Examples include schools, churches, clubs and fraternities. As we become more set in our beliefs and opinions, they become more entwined with our identities as we seek to define who we are and where we fit into the world around us as participants within the community and society at large.

We may join groups of other people who share a similar world view as this helps validate our own understanding of the world. They serve to reinforce our reality. Our perceptual tools evolve to identify the events in our lives that might further reinforce that we are on the right track. All this confirmation allows us to more easily dismiss conflicting information because we have all the proof we need with regard to its accuracy. Every person, every institution who was part of our education has added to the construction—the ego structure that dominates how we define ourselves. When someone asks us to tell them about ourselves, we describe the basic understanding we have about the identity we have crafted to navigate through the human experience—our name, where we live, where we were born, the school we attended, what we like to do, and our job. As we get to know them better, we may share more personal things about ourselves, about our history and preferences.

My own awakening, in connection with a near-death experience, beginning in 1987 and continuing for the next twelve years, kicked off with a revelation in which I experienced myself as who I really was, and still am, a totality beyond the ego-based identity I presented to the world. Prior to that, I had bought into the entirety of who I *thought* I was. Since then I have met many people who have come to the same experiential understanding presented through the near-death experience where, like myself, they were given a glimpse of the true nature of human life that, despite the best intentions of parents and teachers, they were simply not provided.

What I was exposed to during my encounter with the true self is that we are so much more than we think we are. We possess powerful abilities that we use every day, whether we are conscious of it or not. We are powerful creators within our reality. What is to be presented is not new information. The knowledge of who we really are and what we are capable of has been known throughout human history by individuals and secret societies who passed the knowledge along to their initiates.

The need to keep the information hidden was due to the threat of loss of reputation—and sometimes even of life itself—for those who might otherwise have been inclined to share it broadly with the world. Historically, institutions of authority haven't taken too kindly to having their power usurped. Jesus, in The Sermon on the Mount, tried to describe the deeper reality to those attending that day, and it led later to his execution. The interpretation of his message was misunderstood as it was filtered through the belief systems of those who wrote about his life and teachings.

The truth is that whether or not people are talking about it publicly, big questions lurk in the psyche of most of us, waiting to be summoned. In studies of the human genome, it has been postulated that there is genetic predisposition towards the desire for deeper self-discovery and reflection on the nature of our existence. The gene identified as VMAT2 referred to as the "God gene" by Dean Hamer, director of the Gene Structure and Regulation Unit at the U.S. Cancer Institute.

In his book, *The God Gene: How Faith is Hardwired into our Genes*, he puts forth a controversial theory stating that this particular gene predisposes human beings towards spiritual or mystical experiences—and it is the reason we seek out a deeper meaning in life. It could just as easily be called the curiosity gene, as it is fairly common for humans to seek answers to basic questions such as *Where did we come from? Why am I here?* and *Where do I go when I die?*

Some people ask these questions earlier in life than others do. Sometimes they are stimulated by a life event that shakes up the fallback explanations we have become accustomed to. Some are catapulted into the unknown through dramatic openings, such as when a sleeping dream comes true, or in a near-death experience, or when a lost loved one suddenly shows up in the middle of the night.

Other catalysts can be subtler: the onset of an illness, or divorce, loss of income, addiction or depression. Such events can awaken an awareness that what we have been doing is not working, and there must be something else. These experiences can make us feel lost, helpless or angry, yet they are also important in our evolution. They can be a great gift if we are open to the real message they bring to us. There is a certain point when we surrender the notion that we have all the answers and start looking around for other options.

We may be close to doing this very thing on a mass scale, and it would be unprecedented in human history. It could be argued that the inhabitants of this planet are currently experiencing what amounts to an existential crisis, where we realize that the way we are doing things is not working. Scientists, with environmentalists, governments and billions of concerned people, acknowledge for the first time that we may be burning down our home planet and making it uninhabitable. It is happening much more quickly than the most conservative scientific estimates predicted. This is the real thing. The difficulty in grasping the idea of the end of life as we know it is perfectly understandable and yet it is hard for many people to wrap their heads around it.

I thought a lot about how to explain my research and experience as to how everything works here on Earth. In the acknowledgment section of the book, I list some of the thought leaders who are working to help the planet awaken to a deeper understanding of reality. I recommend their books for digging deeper into the information presented here.

In the section below can be found some of what we humans should be told when we arrive here for our Earth experience. It may come across as counter-intuitive, bumping up against everything that you currently believe or think you understand about the world. Take from it ideas that you might want to experiment with, or nothing at all. That's the beauty of the Earth experience: we get to make the choices.

- There is absolutely nothing we can do that will remove us from the encompassing field of love energy.
- There is nothing that we have to perform to be included in that same energy field.
- The power to create is found in the intention behind our actions.
- There is no judgement, and so there is nothing to be forgiven for.
- We came to this plane to learn and play in the Earth school. This is not our home—we are visitors.
- We can't really do the human experience wrongly, no matter what we do. Judgement doesn't exist outside of the human experience. It's all okay.
- Everything on the planet is conscious on some level and possesses a level of self-awareness, though it may not resemble what we are familiar with.
- We are connected through consciousness to everything that exists in our world, and on some level, we experience it even if it occurs to people we will never meet on the other side of the planet.

- We are powerful beyond our ability to grasp and are imbued with an ability to create anything and everything through our will, thoughts and emotions.
- There is absolutely nothing in our lives that we haven't brought to ourselves for the purpose of learning.
- There are many things we can choose to pursue while we are here, but the master lessons to be learned are unconditional love, acceptance and compassion for oneself and for others.
- Every person we encounter while here mirrors some aspect of ourselves that we can learn from.
- Many of us have visited here more than once, and everything we have learned is stored in our DNA and it can be accessed.
- Consciousness exists outside of the human brain.
- It is an illusion that anything is separate from anything else on an energetic level.
- It is impossible to die in the sense that we cease to be. Consciousness is eternal and it cannot be destroyed.
- We experience our reality through physical senses that are attuned to the vibrational frequencies of the Earth reality. It is just a speck of the greater reality we are surrounded by.
- Whatever action we exercise toward another, we experience ourselves.
- What we define as failure is often a necessary part of discovering what we want to learn.
- Our bodies and minds are a receiver designed to capture the vibrational frequencies contained within all that we perceive.
- The highest vibrational frequencies are contained in what we call *love*. Humor is not far behind.
- Consciousness is the animating and connecting force in everything.

- Matter appears solid because its vibrational frequency is slower—just as ice molecules move slower than steam.
- Every thought and emotion we have creates something within the energetic field that surrounds us. Every thought and emotion is felt on some level by others.
- Our current, future and past selves exist right now.
- Everyone in our life is there by invitation.
- Every experience is there by invitation.
- When we judge something, we fix it in place until judgement is released.
- All events are neutral. What we call good and bad are only judgements.
- Everything is vibration. What we call 'God' is consciousness. Consciousness animates absolutely everything in the universe.
- Our physical cells vibrate in coordination and harmony with the frequency of our thoughts and emotions.
- Our genes contain the programming for our human experience. Genes are not fixed—they change and evolve constantly.
- Every action, thought and emotion that we have impacts the world around us.
- What we believe to be true leads to life situations that conform to that belief.
- The conscious mind, or the ego, is a tool designed to assist us as we participate in the Earth experience.
- The unconscious mind contains programming from accumulated experience and it dominates our decisions and actions.
- The unconscious mind is the servant. It seeks to create the human experience through commands from the thoughts and emotions we produce.

- The unconscious mind reacts to every thought as a command. It doesn't understand a command to *not* do or *not* want.
- The energy of every thought that has ever taken place still exists and will do so for eternity.
- All humans share an unconscious common connection with all life forms on this planet.
- All knowledge, even that in what we call the future, is available to be utilized.
- When we enter into lower vibrational activities, such as war, discrimination or injustice, it lowers the vibrations for all of Earth's inhabitants. Acts of compassion, love and acceptance raise the vibrations for all.
- Everything we experience we helped create on some level for the purpose of learning. Every person who shows up in our life is there to collaborate with us and teach us more about who we are.

Chapter 8

Perception, Belief and Reality

"No one can be told what the Matrix is. You have to see it for yourself. The Matrix is the world that has been pulled over your eyes to blind you to the truth. You take a blue pill—the story ends, you wake up in your bed and believe whatever you want to believe. You take a red pill—you stay in Wonderland and I'll show you how deep the rabbit-hole goes."

~ Morpheus to Neo in *The Matrix*

As a child in the 1960s, I would take my transistor radio with me to bed at night. During the daytime, my small radio receiver would only pick up the local AM stations, and I was limited to the same old music, advertising and mundane news around our town. At night, however, something magical happened! A whole new world presented itself, and far away worlds were able to reach out to me. New York, Boston, California and even Mexico were available to me in my little bedroom every night. It was my first introduction to the idea that there might be much more going on out there than I could ever imagine.

I didn't know that the signals from those exotic places were floating around in the air all along. If I had a better radio or the signal was stronger, I might have been able to pick them up during the day too. I was limited in part by my equipment which was designed to receive certain bandwidths within a particular range and distance. At night broadcasters were allowed to boost their signal, and local stations often ended their

Perception, Belief, and Reality

transmissions, making it easier for my modest technology to extend its reach. Every frequency was there all the time—I just needed the ability to tune in.

If you consider that the human brain is a radio receiver, picking up the dominant frequency of our reality, we are partially limited to one station—call it radio Earth. Because we are locked in on that signal, we are not generally aware of all the other frequencies or dimensions of reality around us, just awaiting our interest in tuning in. If we decide to explore those broadcasts, open ourselves to other worlds, we would find that they are often just one click of the dial away.

When we come to the planet for our Earth adventure we are issued some standard equipment that allows us to perceive this reality and interact with the environment we're in. These are our perceptual tools, including our bodies and corresponding physical senses. It takes us some time to get used to learning how to use them and to make sense of the three-dimensional space-time world we have entered into. The equipment is specifically designed for us to navigate and function in this environment.

A good metaphor would be how a computer operates. The complex inner workings of a computer are accessed with an easy-to-use human interface such as Microsoft Windows. This allows us to interact with the processing capability in terms we can understand and extract what we need from the computer. The computer can store our accumulated data.

It can also store a complete copy elsewhere in centralized storage or in the "cloud." It can be accessed for retrieval through a connecting network or the internet. Should we lose our connection or the computer ceases to operate, our data is safely stored in the cloud where it can be downloaded onto another computer or shared with others.

Using this metaphor in respect to consciousness, our consciousness is stored simultaneously within us (local) and in the cloud of universal consciousness (non-local). The understanding that consciousness is not solely a creation of the brain is something that is being studied and validated by researchers at major scientific institutions around the world. This non-locality of consciousness explains why people have experiences of being out of their body during a phenomenon such as near-death or an out-of-body experience.

Our brains and senses are designed to operate within physical reality. Our Earth reality is essentially a holographic structure layered with images, sounds and smells that our senses are designed to perceive and interpret. The eyes, as an example, are a holographic viewing device that operates by interpreting electrical and chemical impulses in the part of the brain designated for this purpose.

The brain helps us to make sense of any image based on what each individual has learned from life. Over time, when we see a tree, we draw on our knowledge and experience of trees. We learn to establish a relationship between what we perceive and the individual quality of everything we encounter via our senses.

A newborn baby experiences the whole world around it as an extension of itself. Its small world is a messy jumble of sensations and feelings for which it has no understanding, so it perceives that everything that is happening is part of itself. Later on, it will be able to distinguish between what is part of it and what is separate. The parents are the first teachers that a baby comes into contact with. Almost immediately they help the baby begin the process of defining the reality and understanding that there is some meaning to what it experienced through its senses.

The interpretation of what we experience evolves as we grow and learn. How we interpret the meaning of things in our life is influenced by our corresponding emotional response to them. There is no fixed meaning to them and, essentially, we are thrust into our own individual perceptual field—the interpretation of reality is totally unique to each person.

For each participant in the human experience, no two people have exactly the same interpretation of reality. Therefore we can only understand each other to the extent that we can empathize, but even that only gets us so far since that also must go through the filter of our personal life-script. When attempting to empathize and respond, we can only draw from what we know or have felt under similar circumstances. Our response may not reach the other person in the way we intended it to. All of us have had our intentions misinterpreted, and it usually confounds us.

I can be at a party and having a great time, where you are totally bored. The party is neutral—it exists in isolation

Perception, Belief, and Reality

from any defined meaning. You may get frustrated with me or think I am wrong about the party.

We are attracted to those whose world view is most closely aligned with our own. It makes us feel less alone and provides the comforting thought that our interpretation of reality is valid. The need to associate with those that share a similar understanding of the world is strong—to the point that we often formalize into distinct groups or tribes that agree with our own viewpoints.

Sometimes these groups take a name and go so far as to dictate that the people in that group must agree to conform. They may draft rules that, if violated, would result in expulsion from the group. There may be attempts to recruit other members to the tribe and to convince them of the shared reality so that the group can grow and maybe exhibit power over those with a different perception.

We compartmentalize our thoughts and emotions into something called *beliefs*. Beliefs become enmeshed in the personalities we have evolved to help make up what we have come to understand as the totality of who we are, and they often dictate the paths we choose to go down and what experiences we seek out. As we will learn in a later chapter about our ability to create reality, what we believe to be true is important.

For the purpose of pure experience, our beliefs have a direct impact on perception. To help the world make sense, our brains filter out much of what is not consistent with what we believe to be true. If you have ever seen a magician's act, you know that they rely on us to focus on *expected* action and result. It is necessary for them to operate outside that expectation, to slip by our perceptual equipment and astound us with an alternate reality—what we call magic. The truth is that this happens to us all the time. Our perceptual equipment was designed to reinforce the way we expect our reality to unfold.

Optical illusions are another example of the brain not handling the ambiguity of competing images. As we view a picture, the brain seeks to find a familiar pattern to latch on to.

For the most part, we are pretty sure that the world we experience is just as it is. Actually, it's highly edited by the brain and senses to conform to what is expected. The narrower and more defined someone's beliefs are, the more limited their experience becomes. Beliefs and world views are consistently validated by the fact that we are filtering our conflicting information or rejecting that which doesn't conform. When conflicting information does break through, it can cause something neuroscience calls *cognitive dissonance*, which causes a pain-inducing state of mind.

The introduction of something that challenges a belief can be confusing and even psychologically painful, which is why we often avoid people or information that opposes our preconceptions, instead seeking out reaffirming data that reinforces confirmation bias. The combination of this conscious act, combined with the natural filters, results in a self-reinforcing loop of reality content.

Our experiences are directly related to our beliefs. If we are not conscious of this, then we are swept along in the current. We experience the illusion of progressing forward when, in reality, we may be going around in circles. Our clue that this might be happening is that the same scenarios pop up again and again.

We might want to be aware of our beliefs. Being cognizant of what we believe will ultimately dictate, to a large degree, our accepted identity and what we experience during our time here. Perception dictates reality. The good news is that, if we are willing to examine what we believe to be true, and we make a decision to modify or abandon some of the fixed notions that only serve to impede our ability to achieve our goals, the world we directly experience can change.

Changing some beliefs can happen in an instant, while others are deeply rooted in the fabric of our identity and can take a long time to change. Just as dropping hot pebbles, one at a time, into cold water will eventually make the water warm, over time our unconscious perceptions will alter, slowly shift, and open to other potentials. We can change our default programming and with it the reality we experience. It does require both desire and expanded self-awareness as first steps. An intention needs to be selected.

Doing the same things over and over again and expecting a different result is obviously never going to work. There needs to be an intervention, and it needs to originate within us. We are the captains of our destinies. Either we take control

Perception, Belief, and Reality

and consciously *make* things happen, or they end up happening to us.

I believe depression can be a gift in some ways. It can be an indicator that we are off course for the purpose we came to fulfill and in the story we wrote for this life. Things not working as we hoped can be a gift. Rejection can be the universe's protection!

Chapter 9
The Non-locality of Consciousness

The cosmos is within us; we are made of star stuff. We are a way for the universe to know itself.

~ Carl Sagan, American Astronomer

In the rather materialistic scientific community there is no equivocation over the accepted fact that consciousness is created by the brain through a complex interaction of electrical and chemical impulses. They can't tell us how the brain manifests consciousness, however.

There is a growing movement in the research that validates theories that consciousness is non-local. This means it's not limited to the brain but is contained throughout the organism extending beyond the confines of the body and brain. The theory that consciousness exists in another dimension, while our brain serves to help unscramble and translate, is something that mystics have long accepted and understood.

In indigenous cultures, shamans who travel outside the body to bring back information to the group are seen as carrying out a necessary component of survival. There are cultures who see dreams as sources of information about the future that can help them avoid impending catastrophic events, solve problems that escape their waking selves and gain understanding about their true natures. Dreams are not restricted by time and space—they operate in another dimension unencumbered by the limits of physical reality.

The Non-locality of Consciousness

In the movie, *The Miracle on 34th Street* there is a scene where the court must determine that Santa Claus exists because the United States Postal Service recognizes him as real, at least legally. The judge has to accept that if the U.S. government recognized the defendant as Santa Claus, then this court must as well.

In the 1970s the United States government didn't need any additional verification to accept that consciousness is indeed non-local. From 1977 until it was terminated in 1995, the Defense Department maintained a clandestine program to spy primarily on the Soviet Union. People who demonstrated paranormal abilities were recruited to be used to spy on our perceived enemies during the Cold War. The program came about in response to a similar program that military intelligence discovered to be going on in the Soviet Union.

The subjects who demonstrated the required skills were given geographic coordinates to search for a designated "target." They were induced into an altered state similar to hypnosis. At no time were they told what it was that they were looking for. Even the people that were in charge of the sessions didn't know what the target or mission was for each session.

When provided with such minimal information a remote viewer, or team of them, would enter an altered state of consciousness and project their awareness using the coordinates provided. The amazing thing here is that their unconscious mind would translate the coordinates and deliver the outbound awareness of the remote viewer to the location. The mission always required that the subject report back what images appeared in their mind, which then could be scoured for relevancy for the purposes of military intelligence gathering. The better remote viewers could see it as clearly as if they were looking at a video or through the lens of a camera.

One of the interesting phenomena they discovered is that sometimes they would connect with events that happened outside the confines of the present time—they were time traveling. To address this, suggestions were introduced to the remote viewer in an attempt to control the timeframe within the mission. If this sounds like science fiction, it's not.

Officials at the Pentagon confessed that such a program existed when it became broadly written about in the media, following a story in the *Washington Post* in 1995 by respected investigative journalist Jack Anderson. In 1997 some of the members of the program were interviewed on CNN's *Larry King Live*. Operating under codename *Project Stargate* in the 1990s, it was being overseen by the Defense Intelligence Agency (DIA) and operating out a military base in Fort Meade, Maryland. For over twenty years, a program existed under the codenames Gondola Wish, Grill Flame, Center Lane, Sun Streak and Scanate, and it was moved around to different military and intelligence agencies in an attempt to hide its existence from the public and lawmakers.

In Faber, Virginia, there is a science and research organization known as The Monroe Institute. They study the non-locality of consciousness. It was there that I met two of the participants in the Pentagon's remote viewing program. Joe McMoneagle was one of the star subjects—the accuracy of his hits was extremely high. He has written several books on his experience.

F. Holmes "Skip" Atwater, an army officer at the time, oversaw operations and training for the military government remote viewing surveillance program. Some of the training of the subjects took place at The Monroe Institute. I visited there as part of my exploration and search for answers regarding my own experiences. It was there that I also met Elizabeth Kubler Ross, M.D. She was attending one of the programs offered there, called *Lifeline*. The Monroe Institute attracts people from all professions and walks of life to study the nature of human consciousness. In the class with me were scientists, business professionals, physicians, psychologists, and people like myself who were curious about the research and findings being explored there.

The Monroe Institute is not some self-help retreat—the researchers diligently pursue their study of human consciousness through rigorous scientific methodology and protocols.

The study of human consciousness and potential has been done at some of the most renowned universities, by serious minded researchers. Here are some of the university-sanctioned programs studying extrasensory and non-local human capabilities:

- Stanford University-SRI International (1972-1980s) Remote Viewing
- Duke University: Parapsychology Laboratory (1935-1965)
- Princeton University: Princeton Engineering Anomalies Research (1979-2007)
- University of Virginia: Division of Perceptual Studies (1967-Present)
- The University of Arizona (2006-present)
- The University of California, Los Angeles (1968-1978)
- Cornell University (2002-2010)
- University of Edinburgh (1985-Present)
- Goldsmiths, University of London, Anomalistic Psychology Research Unit
- University of Adelaide, South Australia: Anomalistic Psychology Research Unit (2003-Present)
- Utrecht University (1953 and 2008)
- University of Amsterdam: Anomalous Cognition Section (1990s-Present)
- Lund University, Sweden

In addition, there are current programs that are studying the nature of consciousness and human potential. They include:

The University of Arizona:
The VERITAS (2006-2008) and SOPHIA (2008-present) Research Programs

The Department of Psychology at the University of Arizona is home to two evolving research projects that go by the titles VERITAS and SOPHIA. They were created with the primary objective of exploring the possibility that human consciousness survives the experience of physical death. From 2006 to 2008, VERITAS explored survival of the personality beyond death, until the decision was made to create a more comprehensive body of research, including broader claims of after-death communication, such as communion with discarnate entities (spirit guides, angels, divine higher power) under the program name SOPHIA.

This ongoing research at the University of Arizona's Laboratory for the Study of Consciousness and Health is serious about understanding the nature of human experience beyond the physical. Their web page can be viewed at:

http://lach.web.arizona.edu

It provides details about the program, and the home page states the overall mission of their research:

"To investigate the role of human consciousness and its potential applications for personal, societal, and global health."

Some of the areas of research the program is pursuing:

- Evolution of Consciousness and Understanding (Universal Hypotheses and Post-Materialism)
- The Role of Consciousness in Health and Healing
- Survival of Consciousness After Death
- Quantum Holographic Consciousness
- Group and Global Consciousness
- Animal Consciousness
- Otherworldly/Higher Spiritual Consciousness
- Universal Intelligence Hypothesis

The University of Virginia, located in Charlottesville, Virginia, houses the Division of Perceptual Studies (DOPS). DOPS is a unit of the Department of Psychiatry and Neurobehavioral Sciences and was founded as a research unit of the Department of Psychiatric Medicine at UVA by Dr. Ian Stevenson in 1967.

Utilizing scientific methods, the researchers in DOPS investigate apparent paranormal phenomena, especially near-death and out of body experiences, altered states of consciousness and psi activity, such as telepathic communication. Visit their website to learn more about the research being conducted at the university.

http://www.medicine.virginia.edu/clinical/departments/psychiatry/sections/cspp/dops/home-page

The Institute for Noetic Sciences

Founded in 1973 by Apollo 14 astronaut Edgar Mitchell, the Institute of Noetic Science is a non-profit organization whose mission lies in supporting individual and collective transformation through consciousness research, educational outreach and engaging a global learning community in the realization of human potential. The Institute's primary program areas are consciousness and healing, extended human capacities, and emerging worldviews.

http://www.noetic.org/about/overview/

Science and Nonduality (SAND)

An organization comprised of leading scientists, philosophers and spiritual teachers who come together to explore a new understanding of who we truly are, both as individuals and as a society. This exploration is grounded in cutting-edge science and is consistent with the ancient wisdom of non-duality, the deep understanding of the interconnections of life.

http://www.scienceandnonduality.com

The NOOR Foundation Human Consciousness Project

The Human Consciousness Project is an international consortium of multidisciplinary scientists and physicians who have joined forces to research the nature of consciousness and its relationship with the brain, as well as the neuronal processes that mediate between and correspond to different facets of consciousness.

    The project will conduct the world's first large-scale scientific study of what happens when we die and the relationship between mind and brain during clinical death. The diverse expertise of the team ranges from cardiac arrest, near-death experiences and neuroscience to neuroimaging, critical care, emergency medicine, immunology, molecular biology, mental health, and psychiatry. You can learn more at:

http://www.nourfoundation.com/events/Beyond-the-Mind-Body-Problem/The-Human-Consciousness-Project.html

Chapter 10
You Are Dreaming

We are such stuff as dreams are made on, and our little life is rounded with sleep.

~ William Shakespeare, *The Tempest*

When I was a small child growing up in Richmond, Virginia, my mother used to sing to me. One of the ditties she would sing was *Row Your Boat*. For those of you who are unfamiliar with the simple lyrics they go something like this:

Row, row, row your boat, gently down the stream
Merrily, merrily, merrily, merrily, life is but a dream.

Though she probably sang this to me hundreds of times, I never really considered the words until later in life when dreams became more of an interest to me. One thing that has become apparent is that truth often comes to us in the subtlest of ways. It can come in the form of a simple song, a movie, conversations with a stranger or words from a book.

Life is but a dream, and I have discovered that it is much more than just the nocturnal events we assume are produced in our imaginations while our bodies are at rest. Ponder for a moment the words of the song, *Life is but a dream*, and consider the possibility that it may extend into our waking hours. We also dream during the day.

When we are asleep and dreaming of events, no matter how absurd, they make perfect sense to our dreaming self. During our waking hours, we also are fully accepting of the reality of all our activities and encounters that we experience. We buy into it, rarely questioning its authenticity. There are hundreds of books on dreams and dream symbols that explain how we can learn more about ourselves and the mysteries of life by learning the symbolic language of our non-waking dreams. Because Freud and Jung included dreams in the analysis of their patients, it has become standard practice for much of the psychoanalytic therapy conducted today.

We have rich inner lives that are hidden from ourselves, and from others, that come out of the shadow to reveal themselves in dreams. Consider the possibility that this could be just as true for all that you experience during the waking hours of the day. Let's call it your daytime dream. In some indigenous cultures, it is taught that dreams are the true reality and it is actually the waking world that is the illusion.

In his books, starting with *The Teachings of Don Juan* published in 1965, anthropologist Carlos Castaneda tells of his adventures in Mexico with a Yaqui Indian spiritual guide named Don Juan Matus. Carlos was instructed in how to navigate through the illusory reality of the dream state that we inhabit during the daytime. He came to understand that we can become adept at seeing through the illusion of that which is all around us and we can learn the language of the symbols that present themselves to us constantly throughout our day. These traditions were handed down over thousands of years, starting with the ancient Toltec civilization in Mexico.

The fascination and the study of dreams have been with us through every age of our existence on the planet. In ancient Greece, for example, dreams were considered an important part of how decisions were arrived at. The wisdom contained in dreams was used to guide not just personal decisions of the individual Greek citizen, but also it was used to decide when to go to battle and other important areas of daily life that affected society at large. Dream interpretation was taken very seriously, and people would visit centers constructed for the purpose of dream incubation and interpretation—the best known being The Oracle at Delphi. To learn more about the history of the study of dreams throughout the world, in addition to active cutting-edge research into this fascinating topic, I suggest you visit the site for the International Association for the Study of Dreams (IASD), www.asdreams.org.

One of the most interesting things I have found in my exploration of dreams is a practice known as *lucid dreaming*, whereby a person can learn to become fully conscious that they are in fact dreaming, during their nightly dream state. The term "lucid dreaming" has been attributed to psychologist Frederik van Eeden and first showed up in his 1913 scientific journal article *A Study of Dreams*. Lucid dreaming involves the activation of the waking consciousness into the dream awareness. This allows the dreamer to take some control of the dream and to interact with dream characters, while receiving information with the possibility of receiving healing of psychological wounds. Many people have probably had the experience of confronting a fearful event in a night-time dream, coming to an understanding at some point that it presents no threat because after all, it's just a dream.

If we accept the notion that the daytime dream shares some similarities to the night-time version, we can then start to see that being awake in the daytime dream can have some important benefits. For someone to initiate a lucid dream, they must figure out how to become "awake" in the dream. This is not easy to do because we buy into the reality of the dream even when some really strange things may be presented, such as horses with two heads, flying cars or dead relatives cooking us dinner. When we arise in the morning, we look back on the oddities of dreams and wonder what they meant, and maybe we ask ourselves how come we accepted such strange occurrences without question.

That unconscious acceptance of the absurd, when it should trigger recognition that we are dreaming, and yet it doesn't, is one of the properties of the unconscious dream state. People who learn to cultivate the skill of lucid dreaming are able to recognize incongruity in the dream and use that to initiate lucidity. Should you ever have a full-on lucid dream, it will be one of those rare events that will stay with you for the rest of your life. It is a profound experience.

When we awaken from our non-lucid dreams, we remember them as flat, two-dimensional images that resemble any memory we might conjure up about the previous day's events. When you become active in your dream, you find that you are transported into a reality that is just as real as the one you are sitting in while reading this text. It is a three-dimensional world that may or may not have any resemblance to any place you have ever seen.

You Are Dreaming

You will meet and talk to people and not have any idea who they are. Again, so I can make this as clear as possible, when you transfer waking consciousness, the same one that you walk around with during the day, into your dream body, you will not be able to tell the difference in the experience of reality that you have during waking hours. You can pick up objects, sit in chairs, open doors and walk down city streets in a self-created virtual reality.

It is so real that lucid dreamers have to test reality to ensure they are in a dream. If I push my finger into a wall, for example, and it penetrates, it's confirmation that I am dreaming. If you saw the movie *Inception*, about lucid dreaming, you will remember that Leonardo DiCaprio's character would spin a top and if it kept spinning he would know it was a dream. I was very happy to see that a mainstream movie addressed lucid dreaming in such an accurate way.

Why would anyone want to learn to do this? One reason is that once you realize that you can exist on another plane of reality, which is exactly what this is, the fear of death can be diminished in a way similar to that shared by people who have had a near-death or out-of-body experience. It is a way to understand that we are more than just our physical bodies. I have found it to be the easiest path to a mystical experience, should the idea of that appeal to you.

Another very interesting thing is that since you are outside the confines of the rules that apply to three-dimensional reality, there is *no time*. This is why a late morning dream can seem to last hours, but when you look at your clock it has only lasted ten minutes. Think of the possibilities when the restrictions of sequential time are removed. Lucid dreamers learn early on that they can will themselves to any place and time they want with eerie precision. I have had thousands of lucid dreams and visited the pyramids as they were being constructed, the Sea of Galilee during the time of Jesus, Atlantis, or ancient Rome.

In part, we can do this because the memory of all of history is embedded in our DNA. I don't pretend to understand how it all works, but lucid dreamers do it regularly, and there are few earthbound adventures that can compare with this, in my opinion. You can visit other planets from your bedroom. Pretty damn cool, I think. To learn more about lucid dreaming you can visit the website www.lucidity.com, home of the lifetime work of Dr. Stephen LeBerge, founder of The Lucidity Institute. Dr. LeBerge earned his Ph.D. in psychophysiology in the 1980s from Stanford University. His topic for his Ph.D. thesis was lucid dreaming. Wikipedia has some interesting details on the history of this topic as well.

Not everyone will want to cultivate the skill of lucid dreaming, and it is not the only means of benefiting from the dreaming that happens at night. Remembering dreams and understanding that their language is unique to you is important as well. Not to do so is to miss a large part of the totality of life.

If you consider that what happens in our waking hours could also be just as rife with information and feedback, it opens the door to the opportunity to be more lucid during the day. Under this premise, symbolism that we associate with the nightly dream could be equally available during the day—it is mainly a matter of taking notice. Just as we might learn the skill of bringing waking consciousness to our nightly sojourns, this skill is just as important during the day as we question the world around us and ask *what does this mean?*

Might I suggest that you consider the possibility that you might be asleep right now, as you are reading this? You are entranced in a dream and everyone around you is a character in your daytime dream and you are one in theirs, interacting with each other like actors in a play who believe they actually are the roles they are playing. They may be mirroring back what is actually going on inside of us.

Now expand this out to include the events in your life, and start to scan your everyday world for symbolism. What does it mean if your car breaks down in a dream? Might the same thing not apply to the car you own? Maybe you weren't paying attention to the grinding noises it was making. The car in your dream, or the one you make payments on each month, can both serve as a metaphor for what we use to get around, our physical bodies. That angry person in your life may be helping you understand that you are holding on to some anger hidden within the shadows of your own personality.

Someone who is fully awake in the dream, day or night, has the ability to change the dream by their actions. When fears are faced, they have a tendency to be removed from our experience or to lose their control over us when they occur.

To walk around during the day and look at everything as a potential dream and to be fully conscious in that waking dream is not delusional, since it is an additional tool for participating in your life. Play around with it to see if it is useful. As with anything, it takes practice, and when your emotions get involved, you will find it more difficult to sustain lucidity. When we become emotionally engaged, loss of lucidity and immersion in the illusion will assert itself. Emotions can be an important teacher and they are critical for self-discovery.

It helps to be able to cultivate the skill of shifting to the perspective of dream interpretation and asking, *Why did I create this situation, and what is this character I am interacting with helping me learn? If I appreciate emotions as an ally, will this be any help in facilitating learning and healing?* Instead of reacting unconsciously to the events of the day and viewing them as inconsequential, you are looking to them for the symbols and information they might contain. A sense of gratitude to the people and situations that show up can start to replace other feelings. Maybe we even begin to see the humor in it.

Learning the language of our dreams and of symbolism that is unique to us can reveal that our days are rich with instructions, hints, humor and opportunities for self-discovery. In a nighttime dream, almost everything unfolds through symbols. A bird flies into the windshield of your car, someone spills coffee on you, the dog barks at you as you are leaving the house, or you can't find a document you need for work. These can all be interpreted as random events with no significance, and some may well be. However, some are trying to tell us something if we want to learn the language of the symbols and pay attention.

It may just be that we are sleepwalking through our short lives here on the planet, so immersed are we in the dream that we fail to notice all the clues and hints that are provided. Something very interesting happens when we adopt the mindset that the events in our lives, even seemingly mundane ones, might have valuable information to convey. Just as physicists have found that the act of observing is the necessary component for reality to reveal itself, the same can happen when we start to notice and scrutinize the world around us for meaning.

When this becomes part of our belief system, events begin to unfold more readily. We are then more conscious in living out our stories, awake in our reality and able to use the information in a helpful way. We become active co-creators in our waking reality, in the same way that we are in our nightly dreams.

To become aware of this is one of the pathways to utilizing our full potential as humans. To be conscious was a major goal we came into the human adventure with. This book, and particularly this chapter, may be a reminder for you to wake up.

Chapter 11
The Illusion of Time

Time is nature's way of keeping everything from happening at once.

~ John Archibald Wheeler, Physicist

The experience that time gives us, as visitors to Earth, is that time progresses sequentially, involving what we call past, present and future. Events in the past are fixed there and they are not malleable; the present is what is happening at this moment, as you are reading this chapter, while the future has yet to arrive and it remains a mystery as to what it might bring. This is the template for the way we see the progression and unfolding of the event platform. It is part of the construct of this dimension and arguably it is an important component of the illusion necessary for the concentrated learning opportunity we have here.

Time serves to help us measure our progress by accessing previous actions, making course corrections and planning for what comes next. It provides an appearance of a stable platform from which to operate. As was addressed in a previous chapter, our brains have been designed like a radio receiver to work within the construct of the reality infrastructure designed for this particular learning environment. It may be unique to the Earth experience. It certainly is at odds with the underlying way the universe works at the quantum level.

Science, particularly the field of quantum physics, has penetrated the veil and understands that time is not fixed—far from it. As Einstein revealed in his explanation of relativity, if one were to synchronize clocks using the constant, finite speed of light as the maximum signal velocity, the result would be that observers in relative motion to one another will measure different elapsed times for the same event.

Einstein proved that people traveling at different speeds will measure different time separations between events and can even observe different chronological orderings between non-causally related events. Though these effects are not detectable in our human experience, the effect becomes much more pronounced in the case of objects moving at speeds approaching the speed of light.

In the observable universe, time seems to slow down for matter. Relative to the high-speed particle, distances seem to shorten. The illusion of sequential time seems to be part of the virtual reality of the Earth experience. In the underlying subatomic reality—the operating systems underneath our physical universe—it is being discovered that all time is actually happening simultaneously. This would mean that the past and future are in flux and can be manipulated by any and all events. There is really only what we call "now", and that definition of time encompasses all events. Our written record and understanding of historical events is static, but history is constantly being altered by the choices we are making right now.

Why might this be important to consider? This means that all events are connected and would supersede the illusion of events being isolated in time. The choices we make at this moment as individuals, societies and countries actually alter the past in such a way to make our path forward into what we call the future more easily obtainable. We have long accepted that our present actions can alter the future. To understand that the future is actively taking place in the mode of producing probable outcomes based on present actions allows us to consider the impact of our choices.

There is the added dimension that the past is also altered in such a way that helps us in the present with fewer impediments to the creation process. Is your head spinning yet? If so, just consider that it is what you decide right now at this moment, and your intentions and actions that come out of that process, where the weight of all outcomes reside. With this in mind, being conscious of that puts you in greater control of your story.

The Illusion of Time

People who watch their dreams closely find that future events often present themselves in our waking world, sometimes in the exact manner and circumstances we experienced in a dream. This is not far-fetched when you consider that, when we sleep, our consciousness is not locked in to assisting us in maintaining our waking state illusion, so it essentially "unhooks" from its mooring and is free to roam into other dimensional possibilities.

Time is an earthly convention and, since all time is happening at once in the quantum world, we are free to tap into its jetstream in altered states such as sleep or meditation. I have had many dreams that are glimpses into what we refer to as the future. This one might convince even the most ardent skeptic...

I was visiting a friend and staying at his home because I was going to a wedding the next day. We went out partying that night and, when I woke up, I decided that I was not going to attend the wedding. I had gone to bed with every intention of doing so, however.

During that night's sleep, I had a dream that I was out with the friend I was staying with, and we met two "stewardesses" which is what my friend called them in the dream. One was a brunette, and one was blonde. In the dream, the blonde woman's name was Carol. They said they were wine tasters "on the side."

When I awoke in the morning, I didn't think much about the dream. I packed up my stuff and headed home, living about 90 miles away in Richmond. My friend said he was going to be up in Richmond that night and if I wanted to meet him I should come to the Tobacco Company Restaurant at 9pm. I agreed. When I arrived, he came out and met me in the street with a big smile, informing me he had met two "stewardesses"!

Remembering my dream, I asked him if one of them was named Carol. He said yes and wondered if I knew them. When we walked in, they were sitting at the bar, a blonde woman, and the other, brunette. Sitting on coasters beside each of them was... you guessed it, a glass of wine.

What makes this dream even more interesting is that, when I went to bed, I was 100% committed to going to the wedding in the morning. Had I done so, that dream would have just have been another odd dream that I would have forgotten long ago. When I changed my plans that morning, the dream took on new relevance. I had two versions of reality to choose from, and because I chose the one I did, the dream accurately depicted a future event. This is not unlike what happens to us every day. We make our choices, and with each decision, a new story unfolds to reflect that choice.

In non-ordinary states, we are not limited by the sequential time barrier that is part of the Earth experience. As I mentioned, when I lucid dream or have an OBE, I can go anywhere in time. I sometimes find myself in what looks like a future Earth and in that time or dimension I am a different person when I look in the dream mirror. In that reality, I have a family and job I know nothing about, but my consciousness seems to be the present version of me. It's not unlike the 1980s television show *Quantum Leap*.

Time travel has long been a subject of books and movies. We are fascinated by the possibility, and it is possible, we just can't take our physical bodies with us... yet.

Chapter 12

Why am I Here?

For much of our lives many of us generally accept that we are here to comply with a standard laid out by our parents and society. The majority of us seek the most acceptable route for being productive citizens and members of our human tribe. We progress from being children, where not much is asked of us except to play and maybe try not to get our clothes dirty while doing it. Expectations are relatively low early in life.

One universal characteristic of children is that we ask lots of questions. As our vocabulary evolves, the questions become more complex, but from very early on, we want to know where we come from. Our parents struggle to answer the questions outside of what they have adopted about the origin of our presence here on Earth.

Children's questions that may seem cute and endearing can become irritating and even intimidating later on. Throughout much of our history, asking too many questions about the wrong subjects could get you into trouble with religious or governmental establishments. This was especially true if the inquiries threatened the existing power structure or proved disruptive to the *status quo*.

Historically one of the great protectors of the *status quo* has been the church. When we look at the very first story in the Bible, it is about the penalties for seeking answers to the big questions. We learn very early on that to question institutional authority can cause problems: "you have what you need to know, so be satisfied with the answer" is the message.

When we move into adulthood, becoming fully-fledged members of society, the pressure to learn the rules and conform increases. It is easier to go along with the program, take the information provided and not ask too many questions. We are provided the template for how to live here by our parents, society, religion, employers, government and to a large degree the media. In essence, we get a progressively unfolding education on what our purpose is while we are here and it generally goes something like this:

> *Go to school*
> *Get a job*
> *Get married*
> *Have some kids*
> *Buy a house*
> *Improve earnings and status*
> *Retire*

Just keeping up with all this is a challenge. The time and effort it takes to live out this life doesn't leave much room for contemplating going outside the lines. It is so easy just to go with the flow, not making too much trouble or asking too many questions. After all, this pre-packaged life-script seems to work, right? Most follow along with it and seem happy enough—or are they?

There is nothing wrong with this script. In fact, this script can include a lot of great things. Children are a joy to most, a fulfilling job challenges us to learn and grow, and there are plenty of fantastic places to visit, there's wonderful food to eat and there are beautiful golf courses to play.

It may be the very script you need for what you desire to accomplish in your time here in the Earth experience. How will you know if it is? One of the indicators is that there is a sense of contentment in your life, accompanied by a sense of fulfillment that you're on track for your mission here.

For some, however, either this script didn't fit, or they tried it and it was simply not fulfilling. This could have been apparent from the beginning, but their attention was elsewhere. Others completed the process and were still left wanting, possibly asking, *"Is this it? Is this all there is?"* Maybe the marriage didn't work out as planned, the kids never call, and the prestigious job ended unceremoniously. In the end a person is left with the feeling that what they came here to do has not yet been fulfilled—the mission yet to be realized.

It has been said that everyone has a talent, a gift that they can bring to the world in a way that is unique to them. We often hear about people who knew what they wanted to do

Writing Our Stories

from an early age and were attracted to a particular activity. This passion can reveal itself in many ways—the arts, music, sports, politics, writing or teaching. Such a sense of purpose can take hold of us early and progress throughout the life of an individual. I was not one of these people—maybe you weren't either.

One scenario—the one that I, myself, experienced—is the one where a person has a life that society might view as success. It's a life complete with financial abundance, all the toys a person desires, time to travel, good health, friends and loving relationships and yet… something crucial seems to be missing.

I think that is one of the benefits of living in a country where the opportunity is presented to potentially have all the things that someone might long for, but still, we experience a sense of feeling incomplete. After we have gone through all of what we thought being in this world was about, we still don't feel completely satisfied—this feeling can lead us to ask some of those bigger questions. So where do we draw that line? Or do we? Losing everything, or having everything, can lead to a similar place in our evolution.

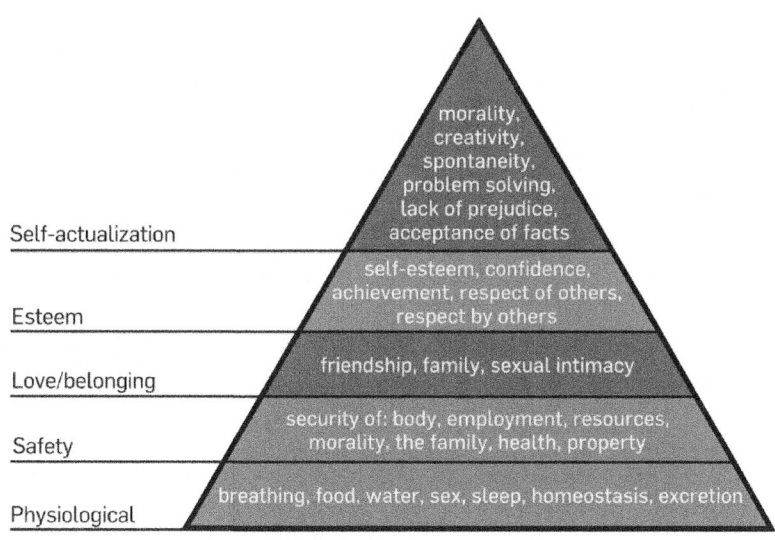

Maslow's Hierarchy of Needs

Why Am I Here? A Handbook for the Human Experience.

Abraham Maslow, a 20th Century psychologist and professor at Columbia University, as well as a number of other esteemed institutions, came up with the Theory of the Hierarchy of Human Needs. Above is a graphic representing the progression from the most basic needs to the pinnacle of what he termed "self-actualization." The premise is that when an individual has met their basic needs, they will logically advance toward higher states of mind and changes in their dominant priorities.

It could be argued that we live in a time when opportunities to have the lower tiers of the hierarchy met are quite accessible, thus opening the door for more people to progress up the ladder and reach more expanded states. In his work he speaks of a possible catalyst for fast-tracking to self-actualization, something he refers to as the peak experience.

Listed below are some of the identifying characteristics of the phenomenon of a peak experience.

- Loss of judgement.
- The feeling of being one whole and harmonious self, free of dissociation or inner conflict.
- The feeling of using all capacities and capabilities at their highest potential, or the act of being "fully functioning."
- Functioning effortlessly and easily without strain or struggle.
- Feeling completely responsible for perceptions and behavior. Use of self-determination to become stronger, more single-minded and fully volitional.
- Being without inhibition, fear, doubt and self-criticism.
- Spontaneity, expressiveness, and naturally flowing behavior that is unconstrained by conformity.
- A free mind that is flexible and open to creative thoughts and ideas.
- Complete mindfulness of the present moment without influence of past or expected future experiences.
- A physical feeling of warmth, along with a sensation of pleasant vibrations emanating from the heart area outward into the limbs.

Asking big questions such as *Why am I here? What is my purpose?* is a way to begin opening to the experiences and states listed above. Because we have free will, it appears that our permission is required for us to begin the process of being supplied with the opportunity to make these changes. In my case, I don't remember asking for this back in 1987, but I definitely had an experience that included and went beyond the Maslow model. I had a turbo-charged version that ultimately changed my entire understanding of reality.

Even though it took me many years to begin writing about it, I needed to test what I had learned. I empathize with anyone who tries to change their behaviors because even though I know all the stuff in this book, I still forget.

As we advance through the process of school, family and job to the degree that we exercise our creativity in unique ways, acting out the script that we have laid out, we find corresponding fulfillment. Our unique footprint is everywhere we have been. No action has been a waste of time.

Everything that has happened was part of the learning experience necessary for us to fulfill who we are today—the richly textured, complex, wiser person that we have become. We maneuver through life with varying degrees of success and mistakes in our search for meaning, fulfillment and happiness. What we might refer to as failure is an important step in the learning process, possibly more important than what we see as success.

Earth is a concentrated learning environment, part school, part amusement park, a Disneyland for the soul. The difference is that when we go to one of the parks and get on the ride, we know that no matter how scary it is, it isn't real. No one would want to get on a roller-coaster that didn't excite the senses. You are a voluntary visitor to a wonderful and at times frightening amusement park called planet Earth.

Part of the admission price is the removal of any knowledge of this fact. Yes, you can get injured while here, and there is both physical and emotional pain and even suffering that is built into the experience. However, nothing happens that does not offer the opportunity to learn and advance toward greater understanding.

The overriding reason we chose to have the human experience is to learn and to love more. One of our most beloved human experience allegories is L. Frank Baum's book, *Dorothy and The Wizard of Oz.* There is a reason many of us watched the movie over and over again—it was because its message was a clue to the mystery as to why we choose the human experience. At the end of story, Glenda tells Dorothy that she could have gone home at any time, to which Dorothy asks why she didn't tell her. Glenda replies that Dorothy wasn't ready for the truth then, and she wouldn't have believed it.

Everything that Dorothy, the Tin Man, Lion and Scarecrow experienced enabled them to find what they were seeking and to bring them to the understanding that they already had everything within them that they had been looking for.

The reason I said that only brave souls come in to play in the human experience is because the rewards are great—we aren't required to exhibit kindness, forgiveness, charity or love. The physical and psychological equipment we are issued when we come into the human experience can just as easily be utilized for cruel, selfish and non-loving acts. *We have the protected right of choice.* Kindness is a choice.

Our lack of knowledge about this choice, and the fact that we still, for the most part, opt to be kind when another option might be easier, is what makes coming to this planet such a coveted experience for the process of soul evolution.

There is also the physical beauty of the world that has been created, as well as experiences that touch us on the deepest level, and many wonderful things that make our time here worthwhile. It could be, however, that the challenges of being human are the biggest draw for some. I suspect souls are lined up to get in here! After all, the world's population has increased dramatically over the decades.

As you contemplate why you are here, it might be helpful to keep in mind that you can't do it wrong. Anything that you orchestrate during your time here goes to the advancement of who you are at the level of your essence, and that is also available to all. What you learn and accomplish is shared with everything.

The master human lessons are to expand the universe and to develop a capacity for kindness, love, gratitude and forgiveness in the face of all odds—odds that often seem overwhelmingly to oppose these qualities.

We learn to express unconditional love, kindness, gratitude and forgiveness in the face of forces that seem to oppose such attitudes. Something magnificent happens across the universe every time this takes place.

Chapter 13
Writing Our Stories

The story of the past doesn't have to become the story of your life.

~ Luminita Suviuc, Author

To participate in the human experience means that we have opted to participate in a story. We are the writer, producer and actor in the story we live out. The plot-lines, characters, setting and what we want the ending to be are all up to us. We design these generally before we come here. There is obviously some improvisation and there are some rewrites of scenes, and some delays and detours that are necessary to stay on track for the desired story outcome. The reality is that we might not finish it in one trip.

A sequel, or many of them, may need to be written to get it all in. This may span a thousand years in Earth time for an expansive tome, or a day for vignettes. When we come here we know the story we have intuitively chosen, since it is also coded into the DNA of our physical bodies. We are constantly being nudged to stay on course to complete the story we came to live. This can come from physical sensations, emotions, events that seem to push back at us and fortuitous events that seem to come out of nowhere. The stories always contain these elements as the prevailing message of the story: love in all its forms—compassion, patience, acceptance and fun.

Fun is a part of it. The desire to play is wired into everyone and everything that is on Earth. If your story has no fun, you are probably not living out your story as initially scripted. Think about it: would you plan a trip that didn't include some fun? You can certainly have a life with zero fun, but that would have to be a conscious decision because it is built in to the human experience.

Characters and Collaborators

We also have collaborators who show up in our lives to help move our storylines along, should we get stuck or veer off course. There is an interdependence with the characters in our story, who are also trying to live out theirs. These are made up of people you know and people you haven't yet met, with whom a pre-arrangement was made to participate in each other's stories. It is not limited to this group however.

We have brief encounters and relationships that can help carry the storyline along. We have a built-in sense of who might be able to assist us to follow the plot, learn the lessons and have some fun with them as playmates. When you accept that almost everyone who has a role in your life may be there because the two of you agreed to be characters in each other's stories, it can open the door to more discovery.

There are also allies who are not in physical reality who assist us as well. These generally speak to us through intuition, dreams and nudges. When you can't find your car keys, it could be that you are forgetful, or that they were moved to avoid a situation that might take you down the wrong road—quite literally.

The Human Story: The Hero's Journey

It has been suggested that there are really only five main storylines in all of literature and film. There are endless variables within those stories, however; the story within the story with a myriad of combinations of challenges to be overcome by the hero or protagonist (derived from the Greek word *argon* or contest); monsters to slay, institutions to oppress, wars to be fought and love to be won or lost. The center of the action is, more often than not, centered around one or more protagonists surrounded by a variety of characters that interact with one another as lovers, villains, friends or figures of authority.

Twentieth-century scholar, professor and author Joseph Campbell's profoundly influential book, *Hero with A Thousand Faces*, suggests the presence of a single multi-layered story from which all dramatic plots throughout human history derive their origin. He called this all-encompassing master story "The Hero's Journey." If you have seen any George Lucas, Steven Spielberg or Disney films, read the *Harry Potter* or *Hunger Games* series, or fairytales such as *Jack and the Beanstalk*, *Alice in Wonderland*, Homer's *The Odyssey* or just about any Tom Cruise movie, you have seen or read the story of the hero's journey. Indiana Jones, Luke Skywalker, John Landon in *The DaVinci Code*, Katniss Everdeen and Harry Potter are examples of the modern-day embodiment of the hero.

Here is a summary of the progression of events that unfold for the hero of the story as they make their way through the cycle of stages of the journey. Included are some examples of the story structure as it is depicted in popular literature.

Call to Adventure - The protagonist or hero is summoned to enter into an adventure or quest. This can come about through circumstances that demand that one must drop the ordinary life one leads. It can also come of one's own volition. In any case, the call will require a change in the *status quo* which will take the hero into unfamiliar territory. Often there is some equivocation or outright refusal to heed the call due to worldly attachments or even a loss of the carefully crafted identity that does not feel that it is up to the task. A good example of this is Dorothy's desire to leave Kansas in *The Wizard of Oz*. Indiana Jones is asked to search for a lost antiquity important to humanity. Katniss Everdeen chooses to take the place of her sister in *The Hunger Games*. In the movie *The Matrix*, Neo is given a choice of taking the red or blue pill. Should he refuse the call and opt for the blue pill he will go back to his ordinary life; however, in choosing the red pill, he will learn just how far the rabbit hole goes.

Extraordinary Aid and Allies - If the hero accepts the call—this can happen consciously or unconsciously—the adventure unfolds. It might appear to the hero that the path is being cleared of obstacles, allowing him to begin. Serendipitous events that may border on the mystical may show up, offering validation of the worthiness of the endeavor. A mentor may emerge in the form of a person, book or, in today's world, a *YouTube* or *TED Talk* video, offering specialized knowledge that will equip the hero with the necessary knowledge, tools and skills to succeed.

Along the way, they may encounter people who are willing to assist in the mission and, in some cases, accompany the hero as an ally. Good examples of this can be found in the movies *Star Wars* and again, in *The Wizard of Oz*. In *Star Wars*, Luke Skywalker received his call to adventure from Obi-Wan. He is sent to Yoda to train in the Jedi arts. Along the way, he enlists the help of Han Solo and others. Dorothy lands in Oz and meets Glenda, a good witch with supernatural abilities who provides her with ruby slippers to protect her on her journey. She meets her allies in the form of a scarecrow, a tin man and a lion, who serve to assist her in her quest to return to her home and loved ones in Kansas.

Threshold - The ordinary world is left behind. The hero has accepted the call and stepped across the threshold. This can represent a point of no return. Past options may be limited or gone, and relationships severed. This is also the part of the journey when reality starts to set in about the magnitude and difficulty of the task at hand. Let's consider the movie *Jaws*: the three main characters take off in a boat to kill the giant shark that is terrorizing the beaches of the sleepy town of Amity Island. At one point the radio and engines are damaged, and there is no way to call for help or make their way back.

Challenges and Abyss - The hero encounters elements of resistance, temptation, complication and interruption to plans that threaten to derail the adventure. The challenges present themselves in all the guises one can imagine and the hero may not succeed at first in overcoming obstacles and ordeals. Allies, skills and tools accumulated are ultimately what extricates the hero, who does not realize that the ultimate challenge, presenting itself as a major loss, has unexpectedly entered the story—one that comes in the form of an attack, injury, illness or death that can end the mission. The hero surrenders to their fate in despair, seeming to have exhausted all available options. All appears lost.

Transformation and Atonement - At the bleakest moment a resource appears that the hero may not even know they possess; an ally arrives to help with rescue, and skills or resources that may have been overlooked are engaged to lift them out of the abyss. The hero, having survived, finds new strength of character and wisdom, and is changed by the experience. The journey, with all its challenges, was necessary for transformation and to gain the reward of knowledge that could not have come any other way.

The Return - Just as they were reluctant to heed the call, the hero may not relish the idea of returning to the old life, to the ordinary world that may no longer fit, following the transformation. Understanding that, the hero returns armed with new knowledge that all may benefit from.

Does any of this sound familiar? It should. There is a very good reason why this story resonates so deep within the human psyche. It is *our* story. It is the one we all share. Those who came here left the other world to answer the call to the Earth adventure—bravely they entered the unfamiliar terrain of our planet, to face the challenges and the abyss. Ultimately, we all return to what is our *real* home, with the prize of what we have learned. It is instantly shared with all the universe. We are greeted as heroes upon our return because we are heroes. All of us, no exceptions.

Only the bravest souls come parachuting into the Earth experience. You are a hero right now, no matter how it might appear to you. The story you have written for yourself is unfolding every day you are here on Earth. To be aware of this is to know that you can edit it, or rewrite any chapter or scene, at any moment. To do so alters the future chapters in that instant as well. Now that you are aware of this, how will you proceed in your story, going forward? What characters do you choose to let go of as they do not fit into the plot? How will your book or movie end?

Chapter 14

The Mirror of Relationships

As we recall the hero's journey, one might logically ask, is there room for a Mr. or Mrs. Hero and some little heroes playing at home? Yes of course! Although the journey is ultimately ours to complete, we can't do it without enlisting others as allies and foils. It takes a collaborative effort since we need each other to help create the circumstances that are optimal for learning and loving.

Getting back to the notion that we are all players in each other's scripts, this reciprocal arrangement to help one another discover what we came here for is an essential dynamic of the Earth experience. We need each other to be a catalyst for stimulating the interactions which prompt emotions.

Our emotions and the corresponding actions that result are the foundation of the human experience. They serve as a key indicator of progress toward our goals through the emotional experiences of anger, joy, hate, jealousy and love. We all agree to be the facilitator for each other's desire to learn by mirroring for the other some aspect of ourselves that we would benefit from seeing projected back to us. We attract the kind of people and circumstances that fit the plot and story we have designed. Unconsciously we are communicating with each other, asking each other below the threshold of conscious awareness, "Want to come out and play?"

This unconscious dynamic of dramatic interactions between participants is what makes the Earth so sought after for learning. Experience comes alive for us in proportion to the emotional punch an experience provides. We categorize emotions as either good or bad, but really all emotions are helpful because they are instructive. Not only that, they provide the flavoring of the human experience. Just as we wouldn't eat flavorless food, we wouldn't want to have a life void of emotion. I doubt anyone would want to join the Earth adventure without it. We are constantly seeking out others with whom to interact. We do this so that we fill our punch card with all the things we want to feel, heal and experience, and that comes most reliably from our interactions with our fellow travelers.

Everyone we encounter shows us some aspect of ourselves. If a person who is angry comes into our orbit, we may be thinking, "Wow, what an angry person!", and we may judge them negatively while at the same time getting angry ourselves. The underlying fact is that, in this particular scenario, both parties agreed to come together for the purpose of teaching and learning about the emotion of anger and to have a chance to transform it into something else. There is now the opportunity to choose to express love, empathy and acceptance as an alternative. It's easier to express love when faced with someone who loves us, and that is far less of a challenge than attempting to love and accept someone who is yelling at you. There is mastery available in every encounter.

All emotions are useful, but only some resonate at a higher vibration. That higher vibrational emotion feels more pleasurable in our human form. It also registers as a lesson learned and it may not need to be repeated. If a person is conscious while in such an encounter, they might have a different take on what is really happening by recognizing that they would not have attracted this situation if it wasn't an emotion they shared. To have mastery of the situation would include being able to feel compassion for an angry person and to be able to thank them for being a teacher. Acts of acceptance, love and empathy are all rolled up in the master lessons we came to experience. Unless we want to repeat it, we may never have to have another angry exchange again, since we won't be sending out a signal to participate in such an exchange.

Interactions with others are plentiful. It could be just a casual encounter where a character briefly enters our orbit. They may be sitting next to us on a plane or have a seat across the table at the local coffee shop. When we move our attention to that person and engage with them, or they with us, there is an opportunity for learning even in that short encounter. We may be looking for a good accountant and it turns out they are a CPA. Becoming conscious of the possibility that everyone that enters our lives could have some information for us allows for never-ending connections that extend outwards exponentially. There is a theory that we are all just six or fewer people away from anyone we might want to meet.

The origin of the "six degrees of separation" theory was proposed in 1929 by Hungarian writer Frigyes Karinthy. The basic premise of this theory is what Facebook and Twitter use to grow their networks exponentially. Technology and the advent of social media opens the opportunity to network successfully with someone who might have the information or expertise we are looking for. The opportunity for emotional connection has been greatly expanded as well. It used to be that, if someone wanted to find a mate, they were limited to a small segment of the population that made up their community. Internet dating can literally open up a world of possibilities for emotional interaction that can last for the length of a lunch, or for a lifetime.

Since relationships are important—if not *the* most important vehicle for learning about ourselves—a variety of encounters can mean a great opportunity for gathering experience, companionship and fun. Everyone we meet can mirror back to us something about ourselves. All the people in our lives contain an aspect of ourselves, should we want to probe to find what that might be.

The Love That Binds

The magnetic pull of an individual we meet is a good indicator of the potential for expanding our self-knowledge, healing and learning. Romantic relationships are one of strongest and most dramatic examples of the feeling of being drawn to someone. It powerfully engages the biological, emotional and psychological programs within us to fulfill one of the purposes of the human experience at its most basic level—procreation.

In an unconscious state, we are susceptible to operating out of our most primal instincts to pair with the best genetic match we can attract. Nature has designed ways for us to find that person. When we locate them, we feel sexual attraction and begin to release a cocktail of natural opiates that grant us a high. This can precipitate feelings and states of being that replicate a mystical experience. When we hear lovers speak, they often use language similar to someone who has had a peak experience. Senses are heightened, a sense of unity between the pair is apparent. When we exist in relationship, everything is better and we are no longer alone. Finally, we have found someone who *gets* us. They love us for who we are, and we feel a complete union.

There can be other dynamics at play as well. It may be that this person will be the one to open us up to unconditional love if that is part of the role that they agreed to fulfill to assist in our learning experience.

Just as likely, they can become a foil, someone who can mirror back characteristics in ourselves that we may be hiding, or that we've disowned, perhaps due to shame. These could be fears or old programming that create conflicts and power struggles within the dynamic of the relationship. If we are not conscious of this, such interactions can continue without abatement until either someone decides to leave, or it is worked through and compromises are made. If we leave and haven't completed the learning, we may continue to duplicate the behavior in future relationships.

If we are awake in the relationship, we are able to identify things that push our buttons about the other person, and often these are aspects of ourselves that we don't appreciate. The person along with the emotions we feel are our teachers at that moment. In the dynamic of the emotional connection and mirroring that takes place between lovers, a profound opportunity for self-awareness exists, and the master lessons of compassion, acceptance and unconditional love are there, if we choose to explore them.

Our parents and siblings are not relationships that randomly occurred: we chose those before we came. This is a hard concept to swallow, for many. In assessing the personalities, life circumstances and location of our birth, some may argue they would never have chosen to associate with those people even for five minutes, much less for a lifetime. But you *did* choose them!

This is amnesia talking. Before birth, we give a lot of thought and planning to who we want as parents. These are the people who will provide us with a foundation and the initial circumstances from which we will be launched into the Earth experience. It is with the full agreement of all parties that this

The Mirror of Relationships

arrangement exists. We agree to play out the necessary parts for one another because there is a mutual opportunity for growth and learning for all. As children, we develop the characteristics and gain some of the knowledge that will be needed to navigate the human experience.

If our life circumstances seem to be lacking in comparison to others, or perhaps we didn't get a good deal in life's lottery, that is because we don't have the benefit of understanding that we have exactly what we need for what we want to accomplish here. The people we call our parents are fellow actors with their own agenda for being here. The children we bring into the world have the same arrangement with us. When they were coming in they knew what they were getting into, just as we did.

We need to honor our children's mission since we have no idea what their path is, or what they want to learn about. It is perfectly understandable that we want to protect them since we see them as a shared aspect of us.

The projection of ourselves onto our children is something that is normal. To be conscious in our relationship with our children is to understand this tendency and to accept their choices. They may appear to not be equipped to handle the world, and we might have an urge to interfere and protect them. This is not always helpful since the pain and disappointment they might experience could be exactly what they need for their learning. Empathy and compassion for others is often learned through these experiences.

Towards a Better Day
Drawing reproduced from *The Story of Life* by Luigi and Kate Agnelli

Just when you think that life has given or taken everything and you can't go on because of the freezing cold and rain, the moment has come to do up that top button on your jacket and continue walking. You must always go on, even if you think you have lost everything, including hope, as in life there will always be a better day. Keep believing this, walk on, and never... never stop!!

Chapter 15
The End Game

I'm not afraid of death; I just don't want to be there when it happens.

~ Woody Allen, Actor/Writer

What happens when we die? This has always been life's biggest mystery and one that no one here can really answer. In reality, energy continues, so we would never really cease to exist, even if we wanted to. The dilemma lies in our understanding of the form that the energy occupies when it is no longer anchored in the equipment, a body, that we use for our Earth experience.

If we accept that consciousness operates independently of our physicality, what we call death is simply an unhooking of the connections that tether our energetic essence and consciousness from their association with the human body. It is the equivalent of an astronaut taking off their space suit. Our bodily suit was in part created by consciousness itself, to provide the necessary vehicle that would be uniquely programmed specifically for our adventure here. All the programming and data obtained during our visit here on Earth goes with us. It has been permanently loaded into our energy pattern and added to the totality of who we are.

There are those who have the opportunity for a much deeper understanding of the true nature of this reality and who can speak about it most authentically. They have experienced what is commonly known as a near-death experience. Due to advancements in medical science and cardio-pulmonary resuscitation, we are bringing a large number of people back from what would previously have been an end-of-life scenario. Many of the people who are resuscitated have a story to tell upon their return that is fairly consistent. Some of the most common characteristics shared by those who have had these experiences are:

- A feeling of leaving the body;
- Viewing the physical body, often hovering above, with an awareness of activity or attempts to revive;
- Traveling away from the scene. Possibly going through a tunnel toward a bright light. Feeling a sense of what they describe as great love within the light;
- Being greeted by loved ones and others;
- There may be a review of the life just lived, and information given about that life, with no feelings of judgement;
- Some see beautiful vistas and hear music that far surpasses anything they have experienced on Earth;
- In some cases, a person is given a choice to return, while others are told they must return to finish their life. They are told that it isn't their time;
- Finally, a return to the body.

It is estimated that about 4% of the world's population has had an experience where a life-threatening situation has stopped the heart and brain activity has ceased to the point where clinical death of the body has occurred. That would account for eight million people in the U.S. alone.

Not only are many of these people having these experiences, but it is becoming common enough that they are offering the rest of us the benefit of hearing about the experience in numbers never before encountered. The originator of the term for this kind of experience was Raymond Moody, M.D. When he was teaching psychology and practicing medicine at the University of Virginia, he encountered patients who would tell him about their extraordinary experiences. They were actively seeking a professional opinion about the likelihood that they might be hallucinating, delusional or, worst case, losing their sanity. He was one of the early researchers on the topic and he published his groundbreaking book, *Life After Life*, in 1975, on the near-death experience phenomenon.

To learn more about NDEs, visit the website for the International Association for Near Death Studies, www.IANDS.org

Dr. Moody was denounced by skeptics, who rigorously sought to debunk his findings. Scientists and the medical community dismissed near-death experiences as mystical encounters, or as hallucinations consistent with the activity produced within a dying brain. Dr. Moody had gone off the reservation as a doctor and a man of science, by suggesting that there was anecdotal evidence of an afterlife. He didn't claim to be anything more than a messenger of others' experiences. He was curious as to what, if anything, this might mean. His work and publications spanned many years and provided answers and, in his view, a satisfactory explanation that we do survive physical death.

Others in the medical and scientific community followed up with similar conclusions. Most notable was respected physician, scholar and teacher Elizabeth Kubler-Ross, who devoted her life to deepening the understanding of what occurs during the process of terminal illness. Her books have been adopted by medical schools and hospices around the world. She spent the latter years of her career helping others better understand what happens when we die.

It was only a matter of time before one of the scientific skeptics would have a NDE experience themselves. Eben Alexander M.D., a highly-respected neurosurgeon with an impressive list of credentials, crossed over to the other side during a prolonged meningitis-induced coma, where brain activity stopped. During that time, he was introduced to a world that was more real to him than anything he had ever encountered here on Earth.

Dr. Alexander had awoken one morning with an extreme headache that progressed to the point that he was admitted to hospital, where he lapsed into a coma. He was given a less than 10% chance of survival. Over a period of days, while unconscious in this state, he was kept alive by medical means. He had left his physical form and was introduced to what he called heaven, where he had a series of experiences that went deeper than most NDE experiences that have been reported.

He recounted his story in a *Newsweek* magazine cover story and in the *New York Times* best-selling book, *Proof of Heaven: A Neurosurgeon's Journey into the Afterlife*, that spent more than fourteen months on the list, selling millions of copies. Prior to his own profound, week-long NDE experience, he had understood his patients' afterlife encounters with the scientific explanations he had been taught by medical science. His logical responses relegated such experiences to a process of dying that produces chemicals whose effects resemble the hallucinogenic N-Dimethyltryptamine, DMT. In experiments, it has been demonstrated that certain parts of the brain could be stimulated to mirror the feeling of leaving the body. This was consistent with the scientific community's rationale that, if it can be replicated in a lab, then that must be the acceptable answer. To argue otherwise could jeopardize one's credibility, if not their career.

In addition to a thriving career as a physician and neurosurgeon, Dr. Alexander taught medicine and surgery at Duke University medical center, Brigham and Women's Hospital, Harvard Medical School, The University of Massachusetts Medical School and The University of Virginia Medical School.

Dr. Alexander states in his books and lectures that his life was forever altered by the event. His previous understanding of the reality he had so comfortably relied on was turned upside down. This is one of the most common repercussions of an NDE, a shake-up of the dominant gestalt, a reordering of well-established meaning and priorities.

It is not uncommon for people who experience NDEs to quit their jobs, leave their mates and generally unhook from the life they had previously known. As priorities shift, so does the very definition they held of themselves and of their life-purpose. A great change results from what was often only a period of minutes spent in another dimension of reality, but it might have felt like hours or days. It is not just the experience of being there in another setting, as much as the encounters, realizations and sensory awareness that dwarf what is available in the Earth experience. Those returning from NDEs come back with feelings, emotions, understanding and knowledge about things that could not be experienced when we are in our physical form.

Part of the frustration that returning NDE experiencers have is the inability to convey the magnificence and grandeur of the experience. The limitations of language suitable for describing the awesome experience make it difficult to relay it to others—making the sharing of it a frustrating challenge. There is nothing similar to compare it with here on Earth, so analogies fall short.

Someone who has had an NDE or any other non-ordinary experience where consciousness has been separated from the body, doesn't have to live with it in isolation any longer. These experiences are getting considerable exposure in the press, movies and books that have been published by researchers and experiencers, and it is nowadays more socially acceptable to talk about these things publicly. For much of human history, people who claimed to have had mystical experiences were dismissed as crazy—they have been ridiculed, burned at the stake or made a saint.

It is understandable that skepticism would prevail since such experiences fall outside of the observable reality that the majority of us subscribe to when forming our world view. Evidence is mounting that there is something to this, which is why research organizations and some universities are studying NDEs and applying as much of the scientific method as possible to the process of determining what can be learned from it. There are simply too many people having these experiences for science to ignore.

There was a time when we thought the world was flat. Eventually, enough people circumnavigated the globe, reporting that this notion was flawed, and we adjusted our understanding to fit the evidence gathered. Eventually we received visual confirmation that indeed we live on a sphere. Still, some believe that the world is flat.

People who have experienced an NDE, along with those who have had other non-local experiences, are the current emissaries of the new lands to be explored. These include people who have had out-of-body experiences (OBE), or gone through verifiable and repeatable tests of *psi* abilities (predicting future events through the use of random event generators beyond the confines of pure chance, or projection of consciousness through remote viewing), and who have experienced telepathy.

Those who, for some reason, have these experiences or possess these skills, want to understand their meaning and purpose as much as we do. As recently as twenty years ago the psychiatric community would have diagnosed these as dissociative disorders, to be treated with pharmaceuticals. To attribute it to anything more than coincidence or hallucination would fall under the auspices of "magical thinking" and treatment would be recommended.

We are entering a brave new world of understanding that we are much more than we ever imagined. Scientists are being forced to become mystics as they explore the unpredictability of the nature of quantum reality. The average person would like to understand more about what awaits them when we die. We would like to know that the people we know and love continue to exist, even though they are not here with us. It may not lessen the grief of their absence, but it will provide some confirmation that they are safe. People who have had the NDE experience help provide that peace of mind.

The phenomenon of after-death visitations is also a subject of study, and numerous accounts have shown up in books and in the media. It is now such a common experience that it can be discussed in casual conversation without someone thinking we are delusional. Dreams when a person who has passed away appears with messages of comfort are commonplace. Such phenomena may be explained away as wish fulfillment or "just a dream." Try telling that to the person who had the experience and you are likely to hear that this was very different to a normal dream.

Hospice nurses and volunteers have long known that, prior to someone's death, they can expect seemingly mystical events. Such experiences are very common for those who work with the dying and often for family members too, and they can no longer be considered an anomaly.

Ultimately, we may be moving toward a new understanding of the end of physical life. We need to start treating it as a celebration, a graduation of sorts, to be acknowledged with the same joy we might have when a family member achieves an award for an accomplishment, or when they have successfully completed their education.

We can be comforted that, when someone dies, they have completed their journey and are going home to sleep in their own bed once again.

Death and Dying in the 21st Century

Physicians such as Dr. Ross, who transitioned in 2004, and Dr. Moody, challenged the clinical community on the treatment of dying patients and on counseling for the families of the terminally ill. They were joined by many other practitioners who were dedicated to a more individualized approach to end-of-life treatment plans. This helped give birth to the modern hospice movement and to palliative care medicine as a recognized specialty.

We now have a new generation of doctors and educators opening further avenues for a deeper understanding about the true nature of consciousness and how we think about death. Dr. Alexander's personal experience, given his professional *bona fides*, lends credibility to the notion that some part of us survives mortality. There are other physicians that have had NDEs and have written books about their personal experience.

>*Dying to Wake Up* - Rajiv Parti, M.D.
>*To Heaven and Back* - Mary Neal, M.D.
>*Return from Tomorrow* - George Ritchie, M.D.

The 2015 cable television series, *Proof* (TNT), was about the near-death experience. The show's premise focused on a medical doctor, played by Jennifer Beals, who lost a child in an accident and was bankrolled for a study by a billionaire diagnosed with a terminal illness to find proof that consciousness survives death. Oprah Winfrey and Dr. Oz have had regular segments on the NDE phenomenon, along with interviews with experiencers. Millions of books have been sold and movies are coming out almost every year that focus on this topic. In a 2014 national poll of 58,000 people, 80% said they believed in an afterlife, up from 73% in 1974.

Dr. Atul Gawande's book, *Being Mortal*, stayed on the *New York Times* bestseller list for much of 2014-2015, for some of that time holding the number one spot. His book focuses on how medicine mistakenly misses the mark by treating only the patient and their illness, not the needs of the actual human inside the body during end-of-life treatment. Given his stature as a physician, researcher and educator (his earlier bestseller, *The Checklist Manifesto*, changed hospital protocols around the world regarding infection control procedures), his book has already impacted the way the medical community treats dying patients. He has given doctors professional cover to abandon ineffective treatments and to help patients better prepare for the reality of their individual situation.

Dr. B. J. Miller is another physician who has dedicated his life to changing the way we view the dying process and treat terminal illness. Dr. Miller, a palliative care doctor and former executive director of the groundbreaking Zen Hospice in San Francisco, suggests that we think of someone with a terminal illness as occupying an inevitable stage of life that most of us will enter into at some point. It is just part of the process of being fully alive.

He shares with Dr. Gawande the idea that medicine's focus on extending life, often piling on treatments that may diminish the quality of life and even prolong suffering, be reconsidered, *in lieu* of making the time left more meaningful and finding closure. To learn more, visit www.ZenHospice.org and watch Dr. Miller's TED Talk.

How we approach the prospect of leaving the planet to go back home is a choice—we don't really die, even if we want to. In our culture, it's almost as if we view death as a failure. I choose to view it as a graduation. I made it through all the trials that life had to offer, I could have done more but I believe I'll have many opportunities to complete any unfinished business, to make alternative choices and to love more. I plan on coming back if I can, not least because you really can't beat the food here on Earth!

Chapter 16
Can You Help a Brother (Planet) Out?

With great wisdom comes great responsibility.

~ Book of Proverbs

You have arrived at the final chapter of this book, possibly the most important chapter, in my opinion. I hope you have gotten some new information or maybe even have had some epiphanies along the way. I wrote the kind of book I like to read—light on fluff, rich in information.

In non-fiction works, authors often use the end of a book to summarize ideas from earlier chapters, ramp the reader down toward a conclusion and maybe present them with some final profundity. Instead of providing closure, I am using the last chapter to challenge the reader to do something with what they have learned.

I have passed on, via this work, a collection of facts and insights that, if you were to dedicate half a lifetime to discovery as I have, you may have been able to accumulate what you found in this book through your own efforts. If I have earned your trust that I am a credible source and the information rings true, then you now possess a valuable gift. It is my privilege to give it all away. After all, what good is knowledge that is not shared?

I handed this over to you with the anticipation that you may be moved to use it in some way that benefits others. Those with an expanded understanding of the true nature of reality and human experience have an opportunity to do great things with what they have learned.

Earth, our fellow human beings and all the life-forms that populate this beautiful planet need awakened people to take action, and we need to do it right now. Many of us walk around thinking that, if we show our concern about a problem, talk about it and maybe read some material pertaining to the issue, that we are doing something about it. This is a delusion.

All our gifts really belong to others, if you think about it. By choosing to read this book and take in these words right now, some part of you may be ready to participate.

Just as the character of Neo in the movie *The Matrix* could have rejected the opportunity to gain the truth, you also have a choice. You can take the blue pill, put the book down and go back to the life you are leading as if nothing has changed. You can pull down the cloak of amnesia and reclaim the illusion that you are less than you really are, or assume the belief that there is not much you can personally do to make a difference in the world. The other option is to take the red pill and see just how deep the rabbit hole goes.

If we look at our lives as a story, there comes a time in almost everyone's life when something happens that presents an opportunity for the main character to step into the hero role, to leave behind ordinary comforts and take action that extends beyond their personal interests.

Joseph Campbell identified this stage of the hero's journey as "the call to adventure." If heeded, personal qualities of unwavering commitment, perseverance and courage are needed. Meanwhile, we need to adopt what Henry Thoreau deemed essential to personal fulfillment, "to live independently of the good opinion of others."

You would need to be ready to accept this mission with the full understanding that nothing is guaranteed. The hero could lose it all and maybe even die in the process—however, the drive to proceed is so strong that none of this matters.

Right now, humanity faces its greatest challenge, climate change. How can we say to future generations that we knew it was happening and did nothing? Our children and grandchildren look to us to take action. All life on the planet is waiting for us to stop destroying their world and killing species in numbers not seen in 65 million years.

Can You Help a Brother (Planet) Out?

If you feel moved to do something about it, to summon your gifts and talents for an important cause, this could be your time to answer the call to adventure, to be a hero.

Climate Challenges Facing Planet Earth:

- Global temperature rise
- mass species die-off
- warming oceans
- shrinking ice sheets
- glacial retreat
- sea level rise
- extreme weather events
- ocean acidification
- decreased snow cover
- population resettlement
- social and economic destabilization
- drought and flooding
- food and water shortages

Scientific evidence for warming of the climate system is unequivocal. Source: Intergovernmental Panel on Climate Change

All major global surface temperature reconstructions show that Earth has warmed since 1880. Most of the warming occurred in the past 40 years, with 15 of the 16 warmest years on record occurring since 2001. The year 2015 was the first time the global average temperatures were one degree Celsius or more above the 1880-1899 average. Source: NASA

Ninety-eight percent of climate scientists agree that climate-warming trends over the past century are very likely due to human activity, and most of the leading scientific organizations worldwide have issued public statements endorsing this position. Source: NASA

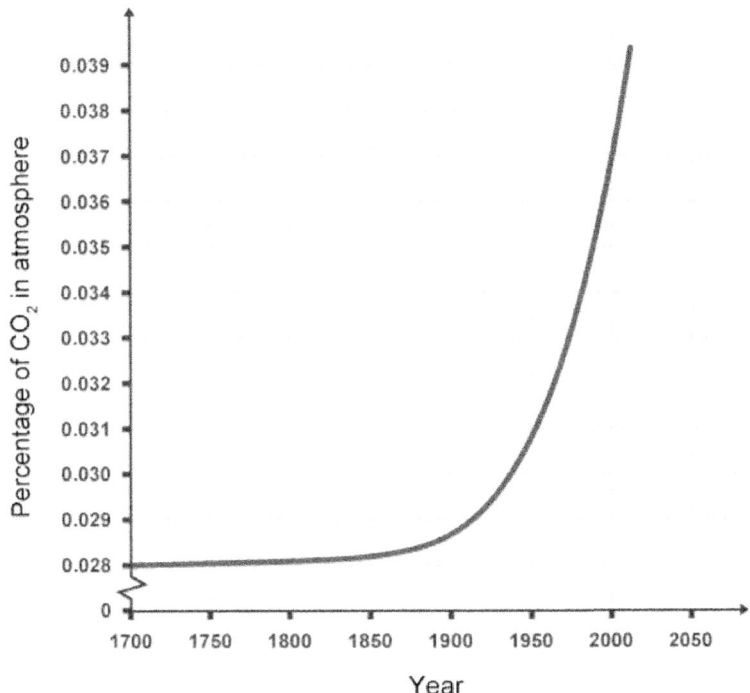

Extra carbon dioxide in the atmosphere increases the greenhouse effect. More thermal energy is trapped by the atmosphere, causing the planet to become warmer than it would be naturally. This increase in the Earth's temperature is called **Global Warming**. Source: BBC.

Source of Climate Images used here: British Broadcasting Corporation (BBC).

Can You Help a Brother (Planet) Out?

Climate Change Facts

- 2016 was the hottest year on record, and heat-trapping greenhouse gases hit their highest concentration ever, surpassing 400 parts per million for the first time in nearly 1 million years. Source: NASA.
- Arctic sea ice coverage has shrunk every decade since 1979 by 3.5% to 4.1%. Glaciers have also been in retreat almost everywhere in the world, including major mountain ranges like the Alps, Himalayas and the Rockies. In 2017, Arctic sea ice reached a record low for the third straight year running, according to scientists. Source: National Snow and Ice Data Center (NSIDC) and NASA.
- Rising sea levels are caused primarily by the added water from melting ice sheets and glaciers, as well as the expansion of sea water as it warms. Levels are currently rising at their fastest rate for more than 2,000 years, and the current rate of change is 3.4mm a year. In July 2016, a massive crack in the Larson C ice shelf finally gave way, sending a 5,800 square km section of ice into the ocean. The newly formed iceberg is nearly four times the size of London. Source: *Wired*.
- The ocean is 26% more acidic than before the Industrial Revolution. The waters are more acidic now than at any other point in the last 300,000 years. The ocean has absorbed about 30% of the carbon dioxide humans have sent into the atmosphere since the start of the Industrial Revolution. Estimated at 150 billion tons. Source: NASA.
- More greenhouse gases are present in our atmosphere than at any point in human history. The concentration of carbon dioxide in the atmosphere reached the milestone of 400 parts per million for the first time in 2015 and surged again to new records in 2016, according to the World Meteorological Organization's annual *Greenhouse Gas Bulletin*.
- More than a million species face potential extinction as a result of disappearing habitats, changing ecosystems and acidifying oceans.
- The current pace of global average temperature rise puts approximately 25% to 35% of plant and animal species at

increased risk of extinction. **We are currently in what scientists are calling the Sixth Mass Extinction, with a species extinction rate 100 times the normal rate.** Source: CNN.

- The Arctic region may have its first completely ice-free summer by 2040.
- The United States is the second largest contributor to CO_2 in the atmosphere, though it is home to just 4.4% of the world's population.
- Average sea level is expected to rise 1-6 feet before the end of this century. Source: NASA.
- In 1910 Glacier National Park was home to more an estimated 150 glaciers. That number has now shrunk to 25, as of December 2016.
- The world's coral reefs are in the midst of a global mass die-off. As of 2015, coral bleaching has impacted 40% of the world's coral reefs, killing over 4,630 square miles of reefs. Source: NASA.
- Climate change is now considered the greatest single threat to the global economy. Source: World Economic Forum.
- Based on current trends and needs, the demand for water in 2030 will be 40% more than can be sustained. Source: Organization for Economic Cooperation and Development (OECD).
- A coalition of 25 military and national security experts, including former advisers to Ronald Reagan and George W Bush, has warned that climate change poses a "significant risk to U.S. national security and international security", requiring more attention from the U.S. federal government. Source: *The Guardian.*
- Studies are now presenting data showing that a combination of increased levels of carbon dioxide in the atmosphere, rising temperatures and changes to precipitation are significantly affecting yields for staple crops such as corn and wheat. This is particularly evident in tropical areas, where food production is normally high.
- Areas that are experiencing increasing temperatures due to climate change will see an increase in attrition due to

insects and other pests. Currently, crop predators are responsible for 25-40% of all crop loss.

What can I do?

- Educate yourself about climate science;
- promote awareness newsletters and social media;
- present at conferences, events, and local library;
- support and donate to organizations involved with climate change;
- start grass roots organizations in your community;
- peaceful citizen activism—contact your representatives;
- make your home green (solar).

For more information about climate science and what you can do, visit:

www.greenenergyproject.earth

Epilogue

For all our perceived individual differences, one thing we share is the human experience itself. I have a theory that only courageous, adventurous and curious souls come to play here on Earth. If we can understand that we are all in this together and that we are linked in such a way that whatever anyone of us feels, all others share in it on some level, we can then begin to appreciate the notion that there is mutual benefit to lifting each other up on every possible occasion.

To the degree that we can accomplish this, I believe that, collectively, we will have reached the highest vibration available in the human experience. Our stories are intertwined with those people we know personally, and they are also connected to the stories of those we will never meet. Be it through the arts, politics or history, we are all in the story of this planet and the experiences it offers.

We all must find our own way to this realization, and it is our own personal experiences that will take us there. Just as it takes a dive in a pool to learn how to swim, we are to dive into life. We may dog-paddle at first, or even sink, and someone has to pull us out, but it is all part of the learning. That is the purpose of it all—to learn. It is really that simple, and life will give us what we have the audacity to ask for.

I wish you a great and wondrous adventure. Live your story well.

Helpful Terminology

- **Classical Mechanics**
Classical mechanics is a branch of physics that deals with the motion of bodies based on Isaac Newton's laws of mechanics, having to do with large objects.

- **Climate Change**
A change in global or regional climate patterns—in particular a change apparent from the mid to late 20th Century onwards and attributed largely to increased levels of atmospheric carbon dioxide produced by the use of fossil fuels.

- **Hero's Journey**
Life's journey as explained in Joseph Campbell's book and in the PBS Series, *Hero with a Thousand Faces*. It addresses the master story of the human condition that makes up most of the storylines found in literature and popular culture.

- **Hospice Care**
Care designed to give supportive care to people in the final phase of a terminal illness and to focus on comfort and quality of life, rather than cure. The goal is to enable patients to be comfortable and free of pain so that they live each remaining day as fully as possible.

- **Intergovernmental Panel on Climate Change**
The international scientific and intergovernmental body maintained by the United Nations and dedicated to the task of providing the world with objective, scientific information regarding climate change and its political and economic impacts.

- **Lucid Dream**
A dream state in which the dreamer becomes aware that they are dreaming, whereupon they find themselves in a 3-D type reality that is similar to waking reality.

- **Many Worlds Theory**
This theory states that every variant of potential at any moment and in any situation breaks off into a separate universe; or, in our case, into a separate world where a version of us exists for every choice we make.

- **Measurement Problem**
The most confounding characteristic of the quantum world for physicists. Particles do not seem to exist until they are measured—that is, observed. The universe essentially is just energy-waves of probability until observed.

- **Monroe Institute**
Human consciousness exploration through the use of technology, education, research and development, for more than 40 years. Founded by Robert Monroe.

- **National Aeronautics and Space Administration (NASA)**
A United States government agency that, in addition to space exploration, conducts research into climate science. This includes monitoring changes in planetary and atmospheric conditions associated with climate change and global warming.

- **Near Death Experience (NDE)**
An unusual experience taking place on the brink of death and recounted by a person after recovery, typically an out-of-body experience or a vision of a tunnel of light.

- **Non-Locality of Consciousness**
The theory that consciousness in human beings exists independently of the physical brain.

Helpful Terminology

- **Out of Body Experience (OBE)**
A sensation of being outside one's own body, typically of floating and being able to observe oneself from a distance.

- **Palliative Care**
Specialized multi-disciplined medical care for people with serious illnesses. Treatment focuses on relief of symptoms and emphasis on the individual patient's needs, with the aim of improving the quality of life for both patient and family.

- **Quantum Entanglement**
Whenever two particles interact with each other in any way, they are forever connected, and whatever one particle experiences, it instantaneously impacts the other one, regardless of the distance between them.

- **Quantum Mechanics**
A branch of mechanics associated with physics that deals with the mathematical description of the motion and interaction of subatomic particles, incorporating the concepts of quantization of energy, wave-particle duality, the uncertainty principle, and the correspondence principle.

- **Remote Viewing**
The practice of seeking impressions about a distant or unseen target using extrasensory perception. Remote viewing was used during the Cold War and beyond as a method of "psychic spying" by military intelligence agencies starting in the 1970s, until it was purportedly shut down in the mid-1990s.

- **String Theory**
The theory that everything in the universe is made up of invisible vibrating strings of energy that exist simultaneously in multiple universes. These are imperceptible to us from our vantage point in a three-dimensional universe.

- **Superposition**
The ability of a quantum system to be in multiple states at the same time, until it is measured/observed.

- **Uncertainty Principle**
(Also called Heisenberg's Uncertainty Principle.) In the subatomic world, it is not possible to predict the actions of particles with any certainty regarding momentum and position. This is an example of the random nature of reality.

- **United Nations**
An international organization formed in 1945 to promote political and economic cooperation among member countries in the arena of helping to build social development programs, improving human rights and reducing global conflicts.

- **World Health Organization (WHO)**
A specialized agency of the United Nations that is concerned with international public health.

Additional Resources

Books

The Dancing Wu Li Masters - Gary Zukav (science)
The Holographic Universe - Michael Talbot (science)
Living in a Mindful Universe - Eben Alexander, M.D. (science)
The Field - Lynne McTaggart (science)
The Bond - Lynne McTaggart (science)
Merchants of Doubt - **Erik M. Conway** (media/culture)
Being Mortal - Atul Gawande, M.D. (medicine)
Many Lives Many Masters - Brian Weiss, M.D. (consciousness)
Dying to Be Me - Anita Moorjani (consciousness)
One Mind - Larry Dossey, M.D. (consciousness)
Seat of the Soul - Gary Zukav (consciousness)
Proof of Heaven - Eben Alexander, M.D. (consciousness)

Documentary Films

Merchants of Doubt (media/culture)
Food Inc. (media/culture)
Chasing Ice (environment)
Before the Flood (environment)
The Cove (environment)
Inconvenient Truth/Sequel (environment)
I Am (consciousness)
What Is Reality (science/consciousness)

ABOUT THE AUTHOR

Mike Marable has been a successful business executive and entrepreneur for the past thirty years, starting his first company, Healthcare Systems, in 1987, and the non-profit venture Human Potentials, an organization dedicated to the advancement of knowledge and personal achievement.

Over the last decade, Mike has co-founded a healthcare technology software company and is currently the founder and CEO of BizVision Consulting, and of an environmental labor of love, The Green Energy Project.

www.greenenergyproject.earth

Mike has been with the love of his life, Gayla, for the past fourteen years and is inspired by her every single day. They live happily in Trabuco Canyon, California.

To contact the author please visit:

https://www.mikemarable.com
Email: mike@mikemarable.com
Follow on Twitter: @mikemarablebook

Sign up for the newsletter and watch for the launch of our world podcast, *Wake Up Calls*.

Mike would also love to hear from you about your own amazing experiences and why you think you are here. A blog is provided on the website so you can share your adventure with others!

Notes

Printed in Great Britain
by Amazon